Sweet & Simple Patchwork Gifts

SWEET & SIMPLE PATCHWORK GIFTS

Copyright © 2006 and 2008 by Boutique-Sha, Inc. All rights reserved.

Patchwork Works (Petit Boutique Series No. 441, 442, 443, 481, 482)
Originally published in the Japanese language by Boutique-Sha, Inc.

English language rights, translation & production by World Book Media, LLC
info@worldbookmedia.com
Translated by Kyoto Matthews
English-language editors: Maureen Clark & Lindsay Fair

Printed in China. For information, address St. Martin's Press,
175 Fifth Avenue, New York, N.Y. 10010.
 www.stmartins.com

Library of Congress Cataloging-in-Publication Data Available Upon Request
ISBN 978-0-312-59136-6

First U.S Edition: March 2012

10 9 8 7 6 5 4 3 2 1

Sweet & Simple Patchwork Gifts

25 Charming Projects
to Make Using Classic Quilt Motifs

HISAKO ARAI AND YOKO SANJO

St. Martin's Griffin
New York

Contents

Simple Squares

Whether you are a beginner or advanced quilter, the projects compiled in this charming book will delight you. The choices of fabrics and styles of designs will inspire you to create not one, but many of the projects included. Starting with a simple square technique, you will stitch squares, four-patches, and rectangles of color into small works of art that make these wonderful gifts:

Coin Purse

Cozy Quilt

Pencil Cases

Shabby Chic Potholders

Placemat

Travel Case

1 Coin Purse

With a curtsy to the past, this vintage-style coin purse transforms the traditional square four-patch into diamonds. Get your scrap stash out and see what treasures you can create!

Materials

Assorted prints
13 ¾" x 19 ¾" (35 x 50 cm) in total

Checkered fabric
9 ¾" x 19 ¾" (25 x 50 cm)

Fusible batting
9 ¾" x 23 ½" (25 x 60 cm)

Lining
7 ¾" x 19 ¾" (20 x 50 cm)

Clasp
One clasp with inner size of 4 ¾"
(12 cm)-wide and 1 ½" (3.5 cm)-long

Cut the fabric.

Trace and cut out templates **A**, **B**,
and **C** on page 10 (following template
cutting instructions on page 107). Cut
fabric pieces adding a ¼" (0.7 cm)
seam allowance:

• 20 **A** pieces of assorted prints
• 32 **A** pieces of checkered fabric
• 40 **B** pieces of assorted prints
• 2 lining pieces using full-size purse
  template

Patchwork Diagram

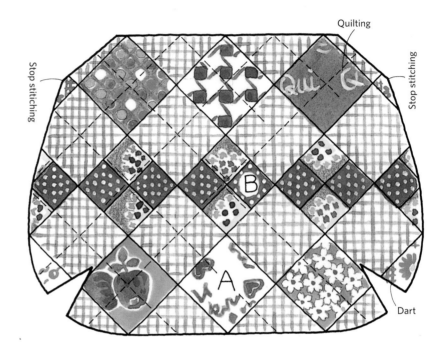

*Sew using a ¼" (0.7 cm) seam allowance, unless otherwise noted.

Sew the blocks.

1. Make a four-patch block by sewing four **B** pieces together. Make 10 four-patch
blocks. Next, using 16 checkered **A** pieces, 10 assorted print **A** pieces, and 5 four-
patch blocks, sew one coin purse top, as shown in the above patchwork diagram.
Repeat process with remaining pieces and blocks to construct a top for the other
side of the coin purse.

Quilt and sew the purse.

①

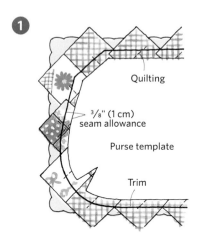

Quilting

³/₈" (1 cm)
seam allowance

Purse template

Trim

②

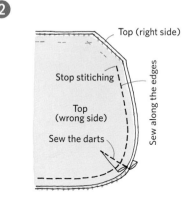

Top (right side)

Stop stitiching

Top
(wrong side)

Sew the darts

Sew along the edges

③

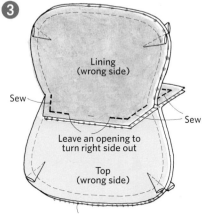

Lining
(wrong side)

Sew

Sew

Leave an opening to
turn right side out

Top
(wrong side)

Top (right side)

1. Press fusible batting to wrong side of each coin purse top. Quilt, as shown in the patchwork diagram on page 8. After quilting, use the full-size purse pattern to trim the coin purse top into shape, adding a ³/₈" (1 cm) seam allowance.

2. Sew the darts. With right sides together, layer the two coin purse tops and sew along the edges, using a ³/₈" (1 cm) seam allowance. Leave the top of the purse open. Repeat this step for the coin purse lining.

3. With right sides together, align the coin purse top with the lining and sew the opening edge. Leave an opening in order to turn right side out.

④

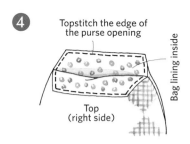

Topstitch the edge of
the purse opening

Bag lining inside

Top
(right side)

⑤

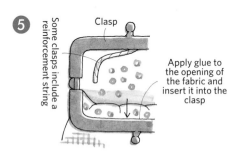

Some clasps include a
reinforcement string

Clasp

Apply glue to
the opening of
the fabric and
insert it into the
clasp

4. Turn right side out and tuck the lining inside. Topstitch ¼" (0.7 cm) around the opening edge.

5. Install the clasp according to manufacturer's instructions.

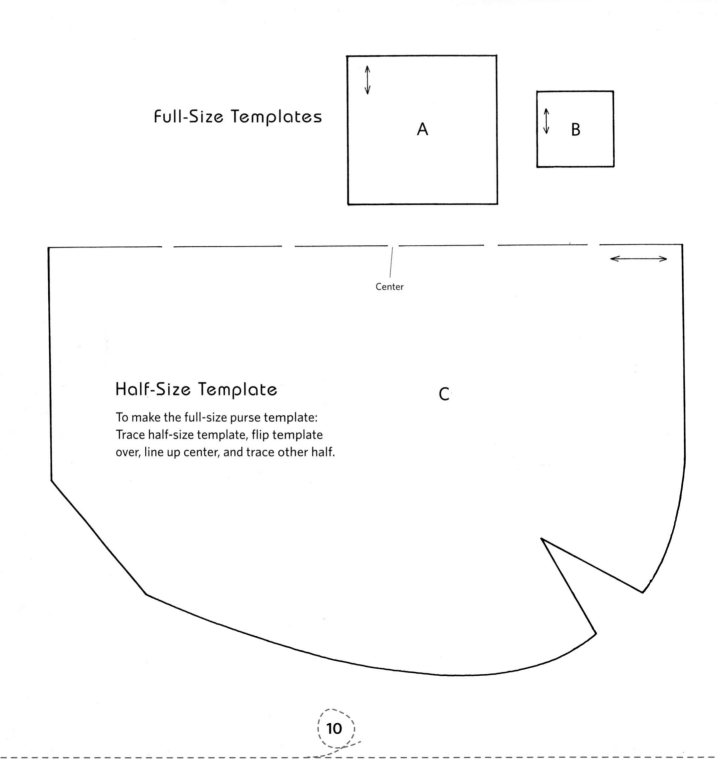

Full-Size Templates

A

B

Center

Half-Size Template

To make the full-size purse template:
Trace half-size template, flip template
over, line up center, and trace other half.

C

2 Cozy Quilt

Add a burst of color to any sofa or table top with this sweet quilt. Its small size also makes it a great baby gift. Simple fabric piecing techniques showcase your design sensibilities in this versatile quilt.

Materials

Assorted prints
44" x 55" (110 x 140 cm)

Batting
44" x 44" (110 x 110 cm)

Backing
44" x 44" (110 x 110 cm)

Binding
29 ½" x 39 ¼" (75 x 100 cm)

Lace
165" (4.2 m) of ⅝" (1.5 cm)-wide lace

Cut the fabric.

Create templates using measurements noted below for pieces **A**, **B** and **C**. Cut fabric pieces from assorted prints adding a ¼" (0.7 cm) seam allowance:

- 16 **A** pieces: 5 ½" x 5 ½" (14 x 14 cm)
- 16 **B** pieces: 4 ½" x 5 ½" (11 x 14 cm)
- 16 **C** pieces: 4 ½" x 9 ¾" (11 x 25 cm)
- Binding: Make a 1 ½" (4 cm)-wide and 165" (4.2 m)-long binding by sewing bias strips together. Refer to page 125.

Patchwork Diagram

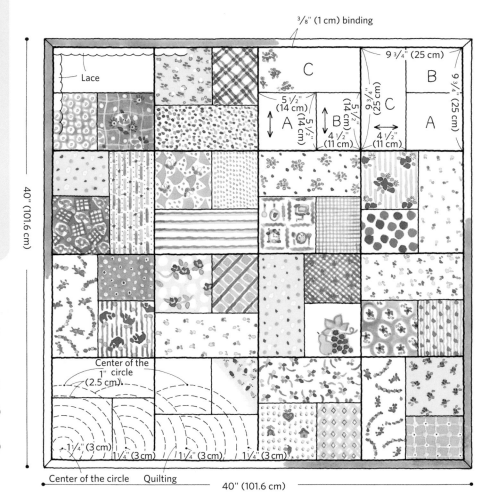

*Sew using a ¼" (0.7 cm) seam allowance, unless otherwise noted.

Sew the quilt.

1. Make 16 blocks by sewing **A**, **B**, and **C** pieces together, as shown in the patchwork diagram on page 12. Next, sew 4 blocks together to make a row. Sew 4 rows together to complete the quilt top.

2. With wrong sides together, layer the quilt top, batting, and backing. Baste and quilt, as shown in the patchwork diagram on page 12.

3. Topstitch lace to the quilt. Sew the binding to the quilt, following binding instructions on pages 124-127.

3 Pencil Case

You're sure to have the most stylish office supplies around with these colorful pencil cases, pieced together with squares and rectangles. One case has a zipper under the flap, while the other has a spring clasp (ideal if you're iffy about sewing zippers!).

Materials
(for spring clasp pencil case)

Fabric a, backing, and casings (plaid)
9 ¾" x 11 ¾" (25 x 30 cm)

Fabric b (pink print)
2 ¾" x 3 ½" (7 x 9 cm)

Fabric c (yellow print)
2 ¾" x 3 ½" (7 x 9 cm)

Fabric d (floral print)
4" x 7 ¾" (10 x 20 cm)

Fusible batting 6" x 13 ¾" (15 x 35 cm)

Lining 6" x 13 ¾" (15 x 35 cm)

Clasp
One 4" (10 cm)–long spring clasp

Cut the fabric.

Trace and cut out templates **A** and **B**
on page 17 (following template cutting
instructions on page 107). Cut fabric
pieces adding a ¼" (0.7 cm) seam
allowance:

- 2 **A** pieces of fabric d
- 2 **B** pieces of fabric a
- 2 **B** pieces of fabric b
- 2 **B** pieces of fabric c
- 2 casing pieces of fabric a:
  1 ¼" x 4 ¾" (3 x 12 cm)
- 1 backing piece of fabric a:
  4 ¼" x 6 ¾" (12 x 16 cm)
- 1 lining piece, cut without seam
  allowance: 4 ¼" x 12 ¾" (12 x 16 cm)

Patchwork Diagram

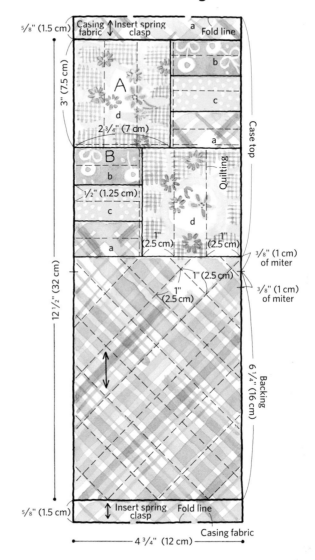

*Sew using a ¼" (0.7 cm) seam allowance, unless otherwise noted.

Sew the spring clasp pencil case.

❶

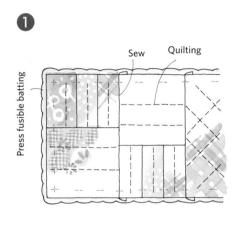

1. Make the pencil case top: Sew the pieces together, as shown in the patch-work diagram on page 15. Sew the case top to the case backing along the short edge. Press the fusible batting to wrong side and quilt, as shown in the above diagram.

❷

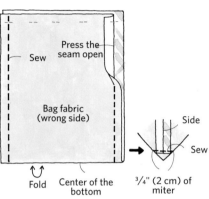

2. Fold the pencil case in half with right sides together. Sew both sides and press the seams open. Miter corners by stitching across each corner at ³/₄" (2 cm).

❸

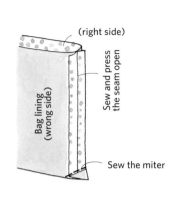

3. Repeat step 2 for the pencil case lining.

❹

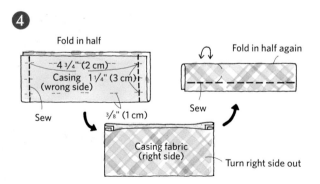

4. Make the clasp casing by folding each piece in half lengthwise with right sides together. Sew both short sides and turn right side out. Fold in half again and sew ¹/₄" (0.7 cm) along the raw edges. Make second casing.

❺

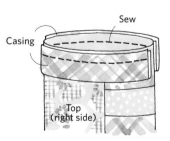

5. Position the raw edges of the casing on right side of the pencil case top. Sew the casing to the top of the pencil case, then repeat for second casing.

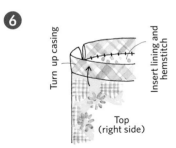

6

Turn up casing

Insert lining and hemstitch

Top (right side)

6. With wrong sides together, insert the lining into pencil case. Fold over the seam allowance on the lining and hemstitch to the case. Insert spring clasp through casings to finish.

Templates

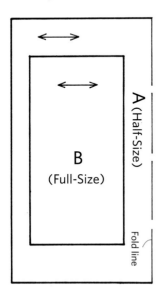

B (Full-Size)

A (Half-Size)

Fold line

Materials (for zippered pencil case)

Assorted prints
9 ³/₄" x 11 ³/₄"(25 x 30 cm) in total

Top fabric (plain beige)
9 ³/₄" x 11 ³/₄" (25 x 30 cm)

Fusible batting
11 ³/₄" x 11 ³/₄" (30 x 30 cm)

Lining
11 ³/₄" x 11 ³/₄" (30 x 30 cm)

Snaps
Two sets of snaps

Zipper
One 7 ³/₄" (20 cm)-long zipper

Button
One decorative button

Thread
6-strand embroidery floss (pink)

Cut the fabric.

Cut two each of flap, top fabric (cut on fold), and lining pieces following measurements noted in patchwork diagram below, adding a ¹/₄" (0.7 cm) seam allowance. Trace and cut out template **A** on page 18 (following template cutting instructions on page 107). Cut 30 **A** pieces from assorted prints, adding a ¹/₄" (0.7 cm) seam allowance.

*Sew using a ¹/₄" (0.7 cm) seam allowance, unless otherwise noted.

Patchwork Diagram

³/₄" (2 cm)

³/₄" (2 cm)

³/₄" (2 cm)

Flap

2 ¹/₂" (6.5 cm)

Position for the decorative button

1" (2.5 cm)

¹/₄" (0.7 cm)

Leave a 2 ¹/₄" (6 cm) opening to turn right side out

7 ³/₄" (20 cm)

Stitch with pink colored embroidery floss (2 strands)

Position of the flap

Opening for the zipper

3 ¹/₂" (9 cm)

⁵/₈" (1.5 cm)

³/₈" (1 cm)

¹/₄" (0.5 cm)

A

Top fabric

Top fabric

¹/₄" (0.7 cm)

Leave 2 ¹/₄" (6 cm) the opening to turn out right side

³/₈" (1 cm)

1 ³/₄" (4.5 cm)

9 ¹/₂" (24 cm)

Center of the bottom, Fold line

Sew the zippered pencil case.

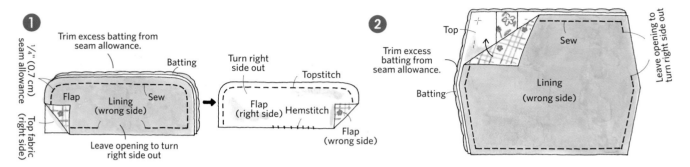

1. Make the flap: Press fusible batting to wrong side of flap. With right sides together, layer the flap and lining and sew along edges. Leave an opening on the bottom. Turn right side out, topstitch ¼" (0.7 cm) from edge and hemstitch opening closed.

2. Make the pencil case top: Sew the **A** pieces together, as shown in the patchwork diagram on page 17. Sew top fabric pieces to each side of the pencil case top. Press the fusible batting to the wrong side of the case top. Layer the case top and lining with right sides together and sew along edges, leaving an openeing.

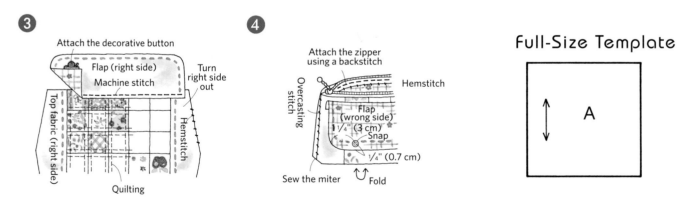

Full-Size Template

A

3. Turn right side out and quilt, as shown above. Use two strands of embroidery floss to quilt flap and top fabric. Hemstitch opening closed. Attach flap to the right side of the pencil case top. Add decorative button.

4. Fold pencil case and sew side seams using an overcast stitch. Miter corners (as shown in step 2 on page 16). Attach the zipper to the pencil case top by backstitching about ⅛" (0.3 cm) from the raw edge of the zipper. Hemstitch lining to the zipper. Add snaps to complete the case.

4 Shabby Chic Potholders

These two potholders are made from the same classic nine-patch pattern, but feature different fabrics. You can customize the design by selecting colors and prints that match your personality—or your friend's personality—which is all part of the fun of sewing.

Materials (for one potholder)

Fabric a (dark print)
6" x 9 ³⁄₄" (15 x 25 cm)

Fabric b (light print)
6" x 6" (15 x 15 cm)

Fabric c (stripe print)
9 ³⁄₄" x 13 ³⁄₄" (25 x 35 cm)

Batting 11" x 11" (28 x 28 cm)

Backing 11" x 11" (28 x 28 cm)

Binding 11 ³⁄₄" x 17 ³⁄₄" (30 x 45 cm)

Leather tie
3" (8 cm) of ¹⁄₈" (4 mm)-wide leather

Cut the fabric.

Trace and cut out templates **A** and **B** on page 21 (following template cutting instructions on page 107). Cut fabric pieces adding a ¹⁄₄" (0.7 cm) seam allowance:

- 5 **A** pieces of fabric a
- 4 **A** pieces of fabric b
- 4 **B** pieces of fabric c
- Binding: Make a 1 ¹⁄₂" (4 cm)-wide and 43 ¹⁄₄" (1.1 m)-long binding by sewing bias strips together. Refer to page 125.

Patchwork Diagram

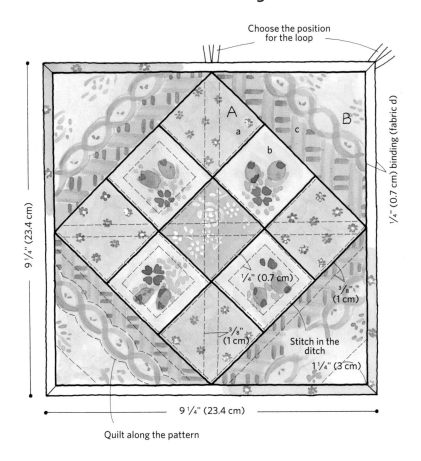

Choose the position for the loop

9 ¹⁄₄" (23.4 cm)

¹⁄₄" (0.7 cm) binding (fabric d)

A

a

b

B

c

¹⁄₄" (0.7 cm)

³⁄₈" (1 cm)

³⁄₈" (1 cm)

Stitch in the ditch

1 ¹⁄₄" (3 cm)

9 ¹⁄₄" (23.4 cm)

Quilt along the pattern

*Sew using a ¹⁄₄" (0.7 cm) seam allowance, unless otherwise noted.

Sew the potholder.

❶

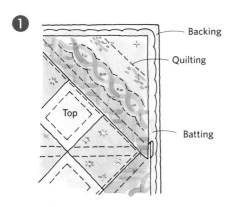

- Backing
- Quilting
- Top
- Batting

❷

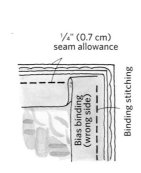

¼" (0.7 cm) seam allowance

Binding stitching

Bias binding (wrong side)

❸

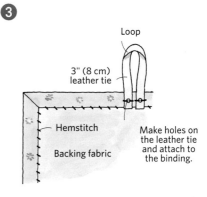

Loop

3" (8 cm) leather tie

Hemstitch

Backing fabric

Make holes on the leather tie and attach to the binding.

1. Make the potholder top: Create a nine-patch by sewing together alternating **A** pieces. Next, sew **B** pieces to each side of the nine-patch to complete the potholder top. With wrong sides together, layer the potholder top, batting, and backing. Quilt, as shown in the above diagram.

2. Sew the binding to the potholder, following binding instructions on pages 124-127.

3. Fold the binding to the back and sew using a blind hemstitch. Attach the leather loop by tacking to the binding to complete the potholder.

Templates

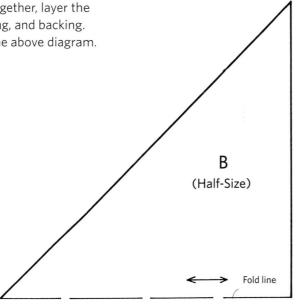

B (Half-Size)

← → Fold line

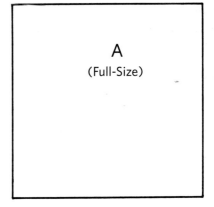

A (Full-Size)

5 Placemat

This mini quilt can be used as a table topper, a basket cover, a wall hanging, and more—a perfect housewarming gift. Simple four-patch blocks are pieced together with squares into a playful design. To add more whimsy, select fabrics in a variety of prints, such as polka dots, checks, and flowers.

Materials

Fabric a (floral print)
19 ¾" x 19 ¾" (50 x 50 cm)

Fabric b (big red checkered print)
6" x 21 ¾" (15 x 55 cm)

Fabric c (small red checkered print)
9 ¾" x 21 ¾" (25 x 55 cm)

Fabric d (polka dot print)
9 ¾" x 21 ¾" (25 x 55 cm)

Fabric e (big blue checkered print)
13 ¾" x 21 ¾" (35 x 55 cm)

Batting
19 ¾" x 27 ½" (50 x 70 cm)

Backing (small floral print)
19 ¾" x 27 ½" (50 x 70 cm)

Binding (small blue checkered print)
15 ¾" x 27 ½" (40 x 70 cm)

Cut the fabric.

Trace and cut out the templates **A**, **B**, and **C** on page 24-25 (following template cutting instructions on page 107). Cut fabric pieces adding a ¼" (0.7 cm) seam allowance:

- 6 **A** pieces of fabric a
- 4 **B** pieces of fabric e
  (Cut these **B** pieces on the bias.)
- 24 **B** pieces of fabric a
- 12 **B** pieces of fabric b
- 30 **B** pieces of fabric e
- 68 **C** pieces of fabric c
- 68 **C** pieces of fabric d
- Binding: Make a 1 ½" (4 cm)-wide and 86 ½"(2.2 m)-long binding by sewing bias strips together. Refer to page 125.

Patchwork Diagram

16 ¼" (41.5 cm)

³⁄₈" (1 cm) binding

23" (58.5 cm)

*Sew using a ¼" (0.7 cm) seam allowance, unless otherwise noted.

Sew the placemat.

1

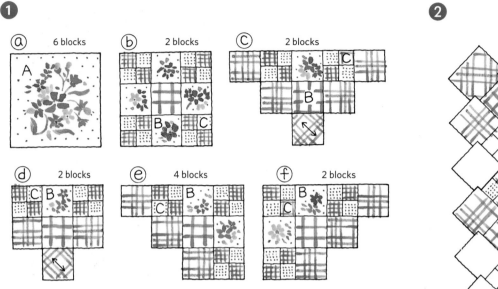

ⓐ 6 blocks ⓑ 2 blocks ⓒ 2 blocks

ⓓ 2 blocks ⓔ 4 blocks ⓕ 2 blocks

2

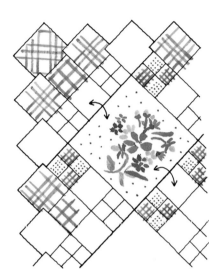

1. Sew the pieces together to create each block (a-f), as shown in the above diagram. Make the necessary quantity of each block, as stated in the above diagram.

2. Sew the blocks together diagonally into rows. Then, sew the rows together, as shown in the patchwork diagram on page 23.

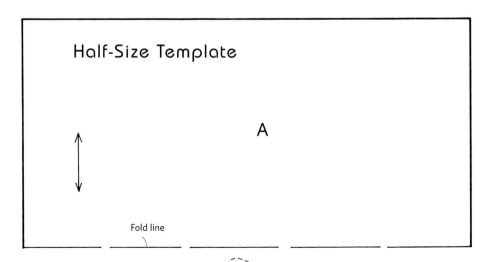

Half-Size Template

A

Fold line

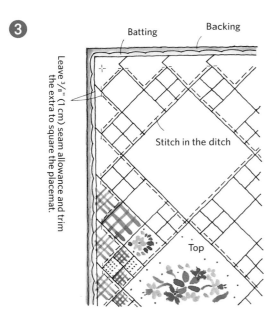
3

Batting

Backing

Leave ³/₈" (1 cm) seam allowance and trim the extra to square the placemat.

Stitch in the ditch

Top

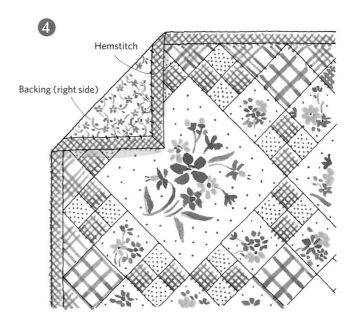
4

Hemstitch

Backing (right side)

3. Square the placemat top by trimming the four sides. Make sure to leave a ³/₈" (1 cm) seam allowance on all sides. With wrong sides together, layer the placemat top, batting, and backing and baste together. Quilt, as shown in the above diagram.

4. Sew the binding to the quilt, following binding instructions on pages 124–127.

Full-Size Templates

C

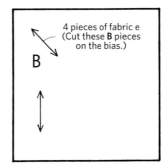
B

4 pieces of fabric e
(Cut these **B** pieces on the bias.)

6 Travel Case

The combination of colorful fabrics and unique piecing is a big "plus" in this design! Piece your scraps together to build a case that will be one-of-a-kind wherever you go.

Materials

Assorted prints
11 ¾" x 21 ¾" (30 x 55 cm) in total

Backing/Gusset (checkered print)
11 ¾" x 13 ¾" (30 x 35 cm)

Fusible batting
11 ¾" x 21 ¾" (30 x 55 cm)

Lining 19 ¾" x 27 ½" (50 x 70 cm)

Ribbon
4" (10 cm) of ⅝" (1.5 cm)-wide ribbon

Zipper
One 11 ¾" (30 cm)-long zipper

Cut the fabric.

Trace and cut out templates **A**, **B**, and **C** on page 29 (following template cutting instructions on page 107). Cut fabric pieces from assorted prints, adding a ¼" (0.7 cm) seam allowance, to make coordinated units a-e.

Cut the remaining pieces adding a ¼" (0.7 cm) seam allowance:
• 1 backing piece of checkered print: 4 ¼" x 8 ¼" (10.5 x 21 cm)*
• 2 lining pieces: 4 ¼" x 8 ¼" (10.5 x 21 cm)
• 2 top gusset pieces of checkered print: ¼" x 12" (2 x 30.5 cm)*

• 1 bottom gusset piece of checkered print: 2" x 12" (5 x 30.5 cm)*
• 2 ribbon tabs: ⅝" x 2" (1.5 x 5 cm)

*Cut additional batting pieces slightly larger than these dimensions

• Binding: Make a 1 ½" (4 cm)-wide and 27 ½" (70 cm)-long binding by sewing bias strips together. Refer to page 125.

Coordinated Units

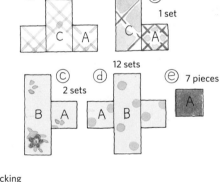

Patchwork Diagram

Case top

4 ¼" (10.5 cm)

1/16" (0.1 cm) stitch

8 ¼" (21 cm)

3/8" (1 cm)

3/8" (1 cm)

Backing

Quilting

¾" (2 cm)

¾" (2 cm)

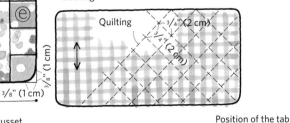

Top gusset

¾" (2 cm)

¾" (2 cm)

3/8" (1 cm)

1/16" (0.2 cm) machine stitch

Opening for the zipper

12" (30.5 cm)

Fold line

2" (5 cm)

⅝" (1.5 cm)

Bottom gusset

⅝" (1.5 cm) stitch

Position of the tab

Ribbon

12" (30.5 cm)

*Sew using a ¼" (0.7 cm) seam allowance, unless otherwise noted.

Sew the travel case.

①

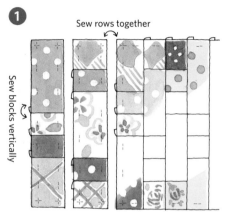

Sew rows together

Sew blocks vertically

②

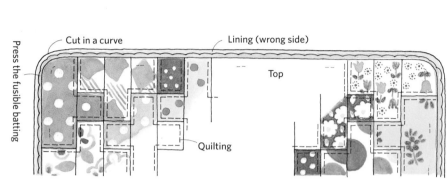

Cut in a curve   Lining (wrong side)

Top

Press the fusible batting

Quilting

1. Make the case top: Sew pieces together vertically, as shown in the patchwork diagram on page 27. Sew the rows together to complete the case top.

2. Press fusible batting to wrong side of the case top. With wrong sides together, layer the case top and lining piece. Quilt, as shown in the above diagram. Trim the corners into curves, as shown in the patchwork diagram on page 27. Repeat this step for the backing.

③

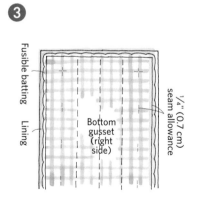

Fusible batting   Lining

Bottom gusset (right side)

¼" (0.7 cm) seam allowance

④

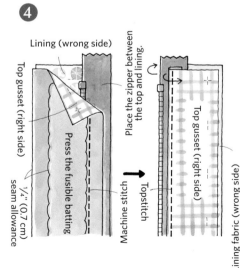

Lining (wrong side)

Top gusset (right side)

Press the fusible batting

¼" (0.7 cm) seam allowance

Machine stitch

Place the zipper between the top and lining.

Topstitch

Top gusset (right side)

Lining fabric (wrong side)

4. Fuse the batting to wrong side of the top gusset. Layer the top gusset, one side of zipper, and top gusset lining. Sew ⅛" (0.3 cm) from the zipper teeth, stitching through all three layers. Turn right side out and topstitch. Repeat this step for other top gusset.

3. Fuse the batting to the wrong side of the bottom gusset. With wrong sides together, layer the bottom gusset and lining. Quilt, as shown above.

⑤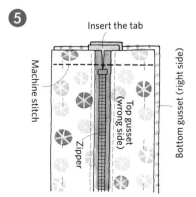

Insert the tab

Machine stitch

Top gusset (wrong side)

Zipper

Bottom gusset (right side)

⑥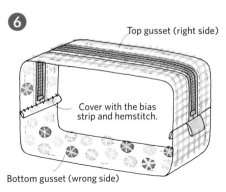

Top gusset (right side)

Cover with the bias strip and hemstitch.

Bottom gusset (wrong side)

⑦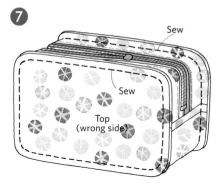

Sew

Sew

Top (wrong side)

5. Close the zipper. With right sides together, layer the top gusset, ribbon tabs, and bottom gusset. Sew across both short ends.

6. Cover the gusset seam allowances with the binding and sew. Wrap binding around the seam allowances and hemstitch to lining.

7. With right sides together, sew the case top and backing to the gusset. When sewing, leave the zipper half-open in order to turn the case right side out.

⑧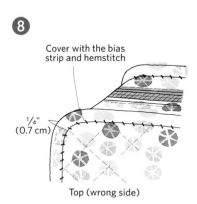

Cover with the bias strip and hemstitch

1/4" (0.7 cm)

Top (wrong side)

8. Cover the inside seam allowances with the binding and sew. Wrap binding around the seam allowance and hemstitch to lining. Turn right side out to complete the travel case.

Full-Size Templates

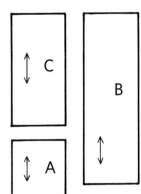

C

A

B

Hexagons

These bold hexagon motifs make an impression, but there is no reason to be intimidated—the size of the projects in this section make working with hexagons a breeze. Easy piecing techniques enable you to create the flowers and honeycombs that shape these cheerful gifts:

Market Tote with Small Bag

Large Wall Quilt

Quilted Throw

Accessories Pouch

Makeup Case

7 Market Tote with 8 Small Bag

Chains of flowers pieced from hexagons adorn this charming tote. Use your scraps to make the matching small bag and you have the perfect carryall for your essentials.

Materials (for market tote)

Accent fabric (linen)
23 1/2" x 27 1/2" (60 x 70 cm)

Assorted prints (12 different styles of print fabric for the flower blocks)
6" x 9 3/4" (15 x 25 cm)

Yellow check
11 3/4" x 43 1/4" (30 x 110 cm)

Assorted prints (for the centers)
9 3/4" x 43 1/4" (25 x 110 cm)

Batting 17 3/4" x 43 1/4" (45 x 110 cm)

Lining/Binding
27 1/2" x 43 1/4" (70 x 110 cm)

Cut the fabric.

Trace and cut out template **A** on page 34 (following template cutting instructions on page 107). Cut fabric pieces adding a 1/4" (0.7 cm) seam allowance:

- 6 **A** pieces of assorted prints (12 different styles = 72 pieces)
- 54 **A** pieces of yellow check
- 40 **A** pieces of assorted prints
- 1 lining piece
- 1 bottom piece each of accent fabric and lining
- 2 handle pieces of accent fabric, cut without seam allowance: 3" x 15" (8 x 38 cm)
- 2 handle pieces of batting, cut without seam allowance: 1 1/4" x 15" (3 x 38 cm)
- Binding: Make a 1 1/2" (4 cm)-wide and 31 1/2" (80 cm)-long binding by sewing bias strips together. Refer to page 125.

Bottom

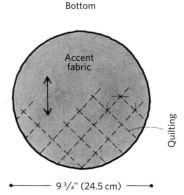

9 3/4" (24.5 cm)

Handles (make 2)

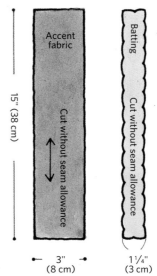

15" (38 cm)

3" (8 cm)   1 1/4" (3 cm)

*Sew using a 1/4" (0.7 cm) seam allowance, unless otherwise noted.

Patchwork Diagram

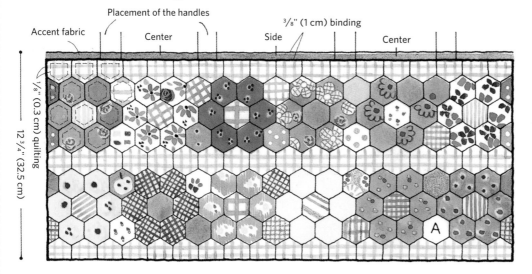

Placement of the handles

Accent fabric   Center   3/8" (1 cm) binding   Side   Center

1/8" (0.3 cm) quilting

12 3/4" (32.5 cm)

30 1/2" (77.4 cm)

Sew the bag.

1

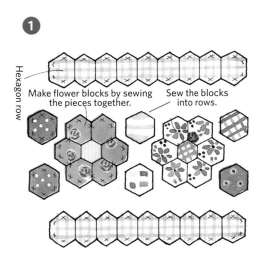

Hexagon row

Make flower blocks by sewing the pieces together.

Sew the blocks into rows.

2

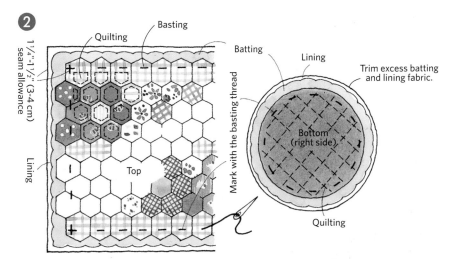

1/4"-1 1/2" (3-4 cm) seam allowance

Quilting

Basting

Batting

Lining

Trim excess batting and lining fabric.

Lining

Mark with the basting thread

Top

Bottom (right side)

Quilting

1. Arrange the hexagon pieces as shown above and sew together. Continue sewing pieces together, as shown in the patchwork diagram on page 32.

2. With wrong sides together, layer the bag top, batting, and lining. Baste and quilt, as shown in the above diagram. Next, with wrong sides together, layer the bag bottom, batting, and lining. Baste and quilt, as shown in the above diagram.

3

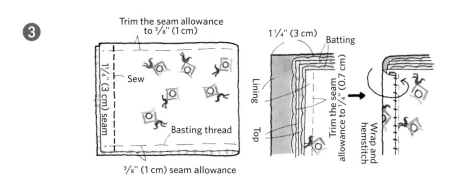

Trim the seam allowance to 3/8" (1 cm)

1 1/4" (3 cm) seam

Sew

Basting thread

3/8" (1 cm) seam allowance

1 1/4" (3 cm)

Batting

Lining

Top

Trim the seam allowance to 1/4" (0.7 cm)

Wrap and hemstitch

3. Fold the bag top in half with right sides together and sew the side using a 1 1/4" (3 cm) seam allowance. Trim top and bottom seam allowances to 3/8" (1 cm). Trim the side seam batting, top fabric, and top layer of the lining to 1/4" (0.7 cm), leaving the bottom layer of the lining at 1 1/4" (3 cm). Fold bottom lining layer, wrap it around the 1/4" (0.7 cm) seam allowance and hemstitch to the lining.

④

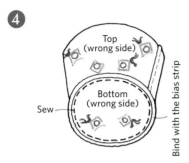

4. With right sides together, sew the bag bottom to the bag. Cover the bottom seam allowance with the binding and sew. Wrap the binding around the seam allowance and hemstitch to the lining.

⑤

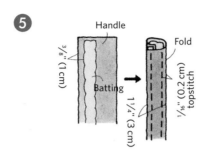

5. Make the handle: Layer the handle batting on top of wrong side of the handle piece. Fold a ³⁄₈" (1 cm) seam allowance on each long side of the handle. Fold in half and topstitch along each edge. Repeat this step for other handle.

⑥

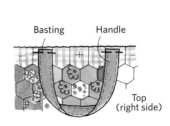

6. Baste the handles to the bag, following the placement guide shown in the patchwork diagram on page 32.

⑦

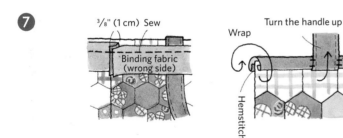

7. Cover the opening edge with the binding and sew, using a ³⁄₈" (1 cm) seam allowance. Wrap the binding around the seam allowance and hemstitch to the lining. Turn handles up and hemstitch to the binding to complete the bag.

Full-Size Template

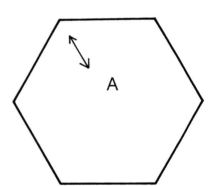

A

Materials (for small bag)

Assorted prints
9 ³/₄" x 17 ³/₄" (25 x 45 cm)

Accent fabric (linen)
6" x 15 ³/₄" (15 x 40 cm)

Batting 8" x 15 ³/₄" (20 x 40 cm)

Lining 8" x 15 ³/₄" (20 x 40 cm)

Clasp
One 4 ³/₄" (12 cm)-long spring clasp

Patchwork Diagram

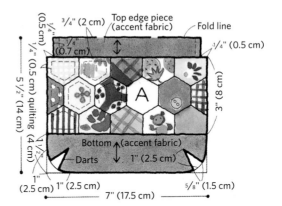

* Sew using a ¹/₄" (0.7 cm) seam allowance, unless otherwise noted.

Cut the fabric.

Trace and cut out template **A** on page 35 (following template cutting instructions on page 107). Cut fabric pieces adding a ¹/₄" (0.7 cm) seam allowance:

- 32 **A** pieces of assorted prints
- 2 bottom pieces of accent fabric: 1¹/₂" x 7" (4 x 17.5 cm)
- 2 top edge pieces of accent fabric: 1¹/₂" x 6¹/₂" (4 x 16.5 cm)
- 2 lining pieces: 4¹/₂" x 7" (12 x 17.5 cm)

Sew the small bag.

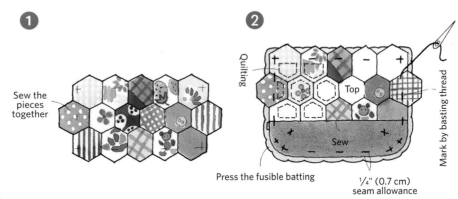

1. Make the bag top: Arrange 16 hexagon pieces, as shown in the above diagram. Next, sew the pieces together, using a ¹/₄" (0.7 cm) seam allowance. Repeat this step to make another bag top.

2. With right sides together, sew the bottom to the bag top. Fuse batting to wrong side of the bag top. Baste and quilt, as shown above. Trim corners into a curve (see patchwork diagram above). Repeat step for other bag top.

③

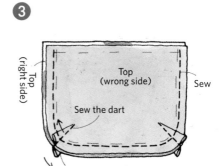

④

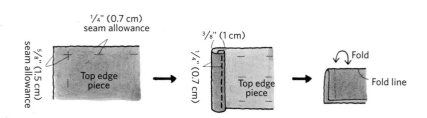

3. Sew the darts on each bag top. With right sides together, layer the two bag tops and sew along the edges. Leave the top of the bag open. Repeat this step for the bag lining.

4. Make the top edge piece: Fold a ⅝" (1.5 cm) seam allowance on each short side of the top edge piece and sew. With wrong sides together, fold in half. Repeat this step for the other top edge piece.

Full-Size Template

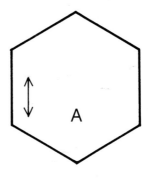

⑤

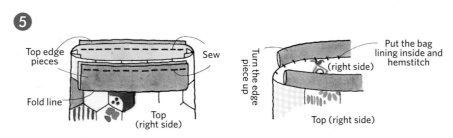

5. Position the raw edge of the top edge piece on right side of the bag top and sew. Repeat for the other top edge piece. With wrong sides together, insert the lining into the bag. Fold over the seam allowance on the lining and hemstitch to the bag. Turn up top edge pieces and insert the spring clasp to complete.

9 Large Wall Quilt

Modern fabrics and buttons give a classic quilting motif a fresh spin in this wall hanging. The bold flowers make a graphic statement—the perfect solution for bare white walls.

37

Materials

*Use fabric a for center of the flower, assorted fabrics b for inner petals, and assorted fabrics c for outer petals in each block.

Blocks 1, 3 & 12
Fabric a 3" x 3" (8 x 8 cm)
Fabric b 6 ¼" x 9 ½" (16 x 24 cm)
Fabric c 9 ½" x 9 ½" (24 x 24 cm)

Blocks 2 & 20
Fabric b 3" x 6 ¼" (8 x 16 cm)
Fabric c 1 ½" x 6 ¼" (4 x 16 cm)

Blocks 4, 17 & 18
Fabric c 6 ¼" x 9 ½" (16 x 24 cm)

Blocks 5 & 19
Fabric a 3" x 3" (8 x 8 cm)
Fabric b 6 ¼" x 6 ¼" (16 x 16 cm)
Fabric c 6 ¼" x 12 ½" (16 x 32 cm)

Block 6
Fabric b 3" x 3" (8 x 8 cm)
Fabric c 1 ½" x 6 ¼" (4 x 16 cm)

Blocks 7 to 10, 13 to 16
Fabric a 3" x 3" (8 x 8 cm)
Fabric b 5 ½" x 9 ½" (14 x 24 cm)
Fabric c 9 ½" x 12 ½" (24 x 32 cm)

Block 11
Fabric a 3" x 3" (8 x 8 cm)
Fabric b 6 ¼" x 9 ½" (16 x 24 cm)
Fabric c 9 ½" x 12 ½" (24 x 32 cm)

Blocks 21 & 22
Fabric c 3" x 6 ¼" (8 x 16 cm)

Batting 27 ½" x 43 ¼" (70 x 110 cm)

Backing 27 ½" x 43 ¼" (70 x 110 cm)

Binding (brown print)
19 ¾" x 27 ½" (50 x 70 cm)

Buttons
Fourteen assorted buttons

Patchwork Diagram

*Sew using a ¼" (0.7 cm) seam allowance, unless otherwise noted.

Cut the fabric.

Trace and cut out template **A** below (following template cutting instructions on page 107). Cut fabric pieces adding a ¼" (0.7 cm) seam allowance:

Blocks 1, 3, & 12
• 1 **A** piece of fabric a
• 6 **A** pieces of fabric b
• 9 **A** pieces of fabric c

Blocks 2 & 20
• 2 **A** pieces of fabric b
• 5 **A** pieces of fabric c

Blocks 4, 17, & 18
• 3 **A** pieces of fabric c

Blocks 5 & 19
• 1 **A** piece of fabric a
• 4 **A** pieces of fabric b
• 7 **A** pieces of fabric c

Block 6
• 1 **A** piece of fabric b
• 5 **A** pieces of fabric c

Blocks 7 to 10 & 13 to 16
• 1 **A** piece of fabric a
• 6 **A** pieces of fabric b
• 12 **A** pieces of fabric c

Block 11
• 1 **A** piece of fabric a
• 6 **A** pieces of fabric b
• 11 **A** pieces of fabric c

Blocks 21 & 22
• 1 **A** piece of fabric c

Binding: Make a 1½" (4 cm)-wide and 130" (330 cm)-long binding by sewing bias strips together. Refer to page 125.

Sew the quilt.

1. Make the quilt top: Sew pieces together into the flower shape blocks. Individual blocks are outlined with a bold line (see patchwork diagram on page 38). Sew Blocks 1-22 together.

2. With wrong sides together, layer the top, batting, and backing. Quilt, as shown in the patchwork diagram on page 38.

3. Trim the excess edge pieces according to the patchwork diagram on page 38 and bind the quilt following the binding instructions on pages 124-127.

4. Sew a button at the center of each block.

Full-Size Template

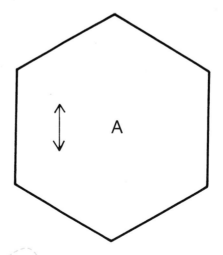

10 Quilted Throw

Diminutive hexagons make simple patchwork flowers in this impressive quilt. Sewing this colorful project is no small feat, but the joy of watching the design emerge like a hidden puzzle? Priceless.

Materials

*Use fabric a for center of the flower, assorted fabrics b for inner petals, and assorted fabrics c for outer petals in each block.

Centers
Fabric a (yellow)
11 ³⁄₄" x 13 ¹⁄₄" (30 x 35 cm)

Inner Petals
Fabric b (27 different prints)
4 ¹⁄₄" x 6" (11 x 15 cm) each

Fabric b (6 different prints)
4" x 4 ¹⁄₄" (10 x 11 cm) each

Outer Petals
Fabric c (27 different prints)
7 ³⁄₄" x 7 ³⁄₄" (20 x 20 cm) each

Fabric c (6 different prints)
4 ¹⁄₄" x 7 ³⁄₄" (11 x 20 cm) each

Borders
Fabric d (white)
29 ¹⁄₂" x 43 ¹⁄₄" (75 x 110 cm)

Fabric e (light green)
13 ³⁄₄" x 43 ¹⁄₄" (35 x 110 cm)

Fabric f (green checkered print)
43 ¹⁄₄" x 59" (110 x 150 cm)

Batting
39 ¹⁄₄" x 47 ¹⁄₄" (100 x 120 cm)

Backing
39 ¹⁄₄" x 47 ¹⁄₄" (100 x 120 cm)

Binding
29 ¹⁄₂" x 39 ¹⁄₄" (75 x 100 cm)

Cut the fabric.

Trace and cut out template **A** on page 42 (following template cutting instructions on page 107). Cut fabric pieces adding a ¹⁄₄" (0.7 cm) seam allowance:

Centers
• 33 **A** pieces of fabric a

Inner Petals
• 6 **A** pieces of fabric b (27 different prints) = 162 total pieces
• 4 **A** pieces of fabric b (6 different prints) = 24 total pieces

Outer Petals
• 12 **A** pieces of fabric c (27 different prints) = 324 total pieces

• 7 **A** pieces of fabric c (6 different prints) = 42 total pieces

Borders
• 286 **A** pieces of fabric d
• 126 **A** pieces of fabric e
• 212 **A** pieces of fabric f*

Binding: Make a 1 ¹⁄₂" (4 cm)–wide and 157 ¹⁄₂" (400 cm)-long binding by sewing bias strips together. Refer to page 125.

*Fabric f (checkered) can be cut along either grain.

Sew the quilt.

1. Sew the pieces into the flower shape blocks as divided by the bold lines in the patchwork diagram on page 42. Make the quilt top by sewing the checkered pieces around the blocks one at a time.

2. With wrong sides together, layer the top, batting, and backing. Quilt, as shown in the patchwork diagram on page 42.

3. Trim the seam allowance and bind the quilt, following the binding instructions on pages 124-127.

Patchwork Diagram

⅜" (1 cm) binding

f

41½" (105.7 cm)

35" (89 cm)

A

a b c
d
e
f

*Sew using a ¼" (0.7 cm) seam allowance, unless otherwise noted.

Full-Size Template

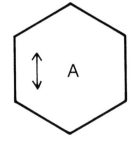

A

11 Accessories Pouch

Hexagon flowers are front and center in this petite carryall. Details such as lace and covered buttons add even more charm and prove that good things truly do come in small packages.

Materials

Top fabric (pink print)
7 ¾" x 13 ¾" (20 x 35 cm)

Assorted prints
  Pink 6" x 7 ¾" (15 x 20 cm)
  Purple 2" x 4" (5 x 10 cm)
  Blue 4" x 6" (10 x 15 cm)
  Green 4" x 9 ¾" (10 x 25 cm)
  Yellow 6" x 7 ¾" (15 x 20 cm)
  White 4" x 6" (10 x 15 cm)
  Orange 4" x 4" (10 x 10 cm)

Batting
11 ¾" x 15 ¾" (30 x 40 cm)

Lining
11 ¾" x 15 ¾" (30 x 40 cm)

Binding (pink checkered)
9 ¾" x 15 ¾" (25 x 40 cm)

Lace
23 ½" (60 cm) of ¼" (0.7 cm)-wide lace

Cording
7 ¾" (20 cm) of ¹⁄₁₆" (1 mm) cording

Zippers
Two 4 ¾" (12 cm)-long zippers

Buttons
Four wrapped buttons
(⅝" [1.4 cm] in diameter)

Cut the fabric.

Trace and cut out template **A** on page 46 (following template cutting instructions on page 107). Cut fabric pieces adding a ¼" (0.7 cm) seam allowance:

- 2 top pieces of pink print:
  3" x 10 ½" (7.5 x 27 cm)
- 12 **A** pieces of pink print
- 2 **A** pieces of purple print
- 6 **A** pieces of blue print
- 10 **A** pieces of green print
- 11 **A** pieces of yellow print
- 6 **A** pieces of white print
- 3 **A** pieces of orange print
- 1 lining piece:
  9 ¾" x 10 ½" (25 x 27 cm)
- 4 circles of pink print: 1 ¼" (3 cm) in diameter
- Make two 1 ½" (4 cm)-wide and 11 ¾" (30 cm)-long bindings by sewing bias strips together. Refer to page 125.

Patchwork Diagram

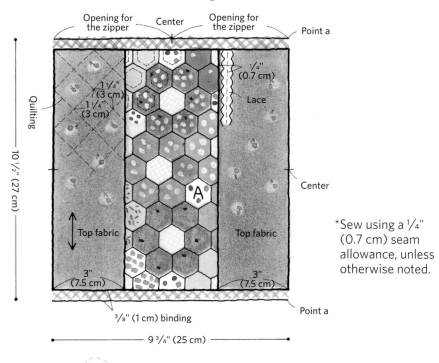

Opening for the zipper   Center   Opening for the zipper   Point a

Quilting

¼" (0.7 cm)

Lace

1 ¼" (3 cm)
1 ¼" (3 cm)

10 ½" (27 cm)

Center

Top fabric   Top fabric

3" (7.5 cm)   3" (7.5 cm)

⅜" (1 cm) binding   Point a

9 ¾" (25 cm)

*Sew using a ¼" (0.7 cm) seam allowance, unless otherwise noted.

Sew the pouch.

1

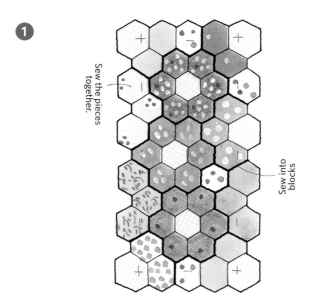

Sew the pieces together.

Sew into blocks

1. Make the pouch top: Sew the pieces together into the flower shape blocks as divided by the bold lines in the above diagram.

2

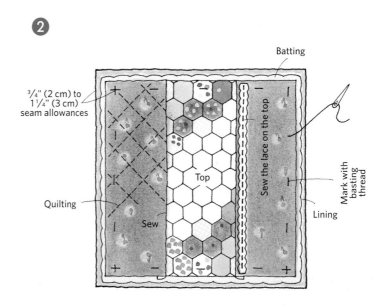

Batting

³/₄" (2 cm) to 1¹/₄" (3 cm) seam allowances

Quilting

Top

Sew

Sew the lace on the top

Mark with basting thread

Lining

2. Trim the pouch top and with right sides together, sew a top piece to each long side of top. With wrong sides together, layer pouch top, batting, and lining. Baste and quilt, as shown in the patchwork diagram on page 44. Stitch lace to pouch top.

3

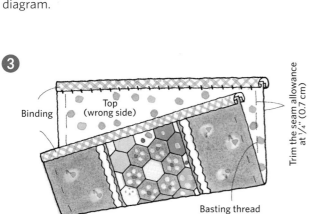

Binding

Top (wrong side)

Trim the seam allowance at ¹/₄" (0.7 cm)

Basting thread

3. Trim the batting and lining seam allowances. Cover the opening edges with the binding and sew. Wrap the binding around seam allowance and hemstitch to the lining.

4

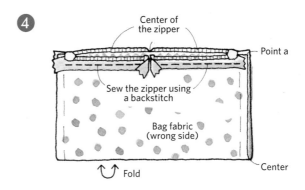

Center of the zipper

Point a

Sew the zipper using a backstitch

Bag fabric (wrong side)

Fold

Center

4. With right sides together, fold pouch in half, aligning point a with point a. Attach the two zippers to the bindings, using a backstitch.

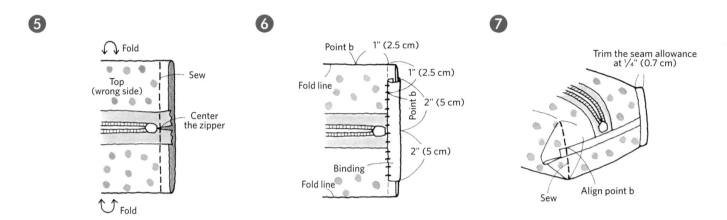

5. With right sides together, fold the pouch so that the zipper is centered. Sew the sides.

6. Using 4" (10 cm) binding strips, bind the area shown in the above diagram.

7. Miter the corners by aligning point b with point b and stitching across each corner. Bind the mitered corners.

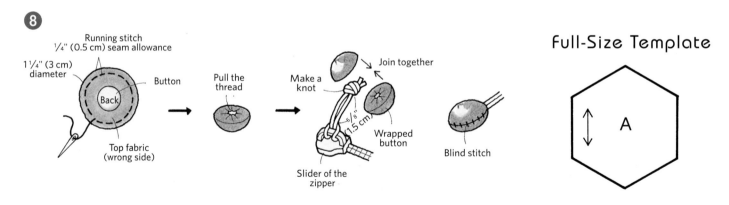

Full-Size Template

A

8. Make the wrapped buttons, following the above diagram. Use the cording to attach the buttons to the slider of the zipper to finish the pouch.

12 Makeup Case

Rows of hexagons are pieced together in this sweet and simple zippered pouch. Add whimsical zipper charms for a double dose of cute.

Materials

Assorted prints
11 ¾" x 21 ¾" (30 x 55 cm) in total

Top fabric (checkered print)
11 ¾" x 13 ¾" (30 x 35 cm)

Fusible batting
11 ¾" x 21 ¾" (30 x 55 cm)

Lining
19 ¾" x 27 ½" (50 x 70 cm)

Zipper
One 11 ¾" (30 cm)-long zipper

Cut the fabric.

Cut two top fabric pieces, and one lining following measurements noted in patchwork diagram at right, adding a ¼" (0.7 cm) seam allowance. Trace and cut out template **A** at right (following template cutting instructions on page 107). Cut 40 **A** pieces of assorted prints, adding a ¼" (0.7 cm) seam allowance.

Patchwork Diagram

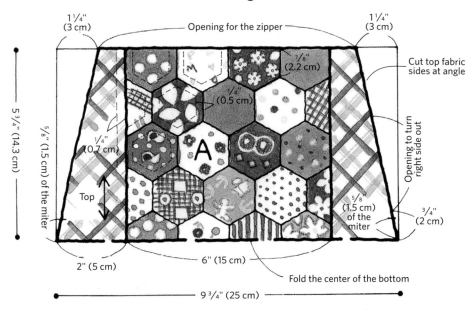

1 ¼" (3 cm) — Opening for the zipper — 1 ¼" (3 cm)

Cut top fabric sides at angle

⅞" (2.2 cm)

¼" (0.5 cm)

5 ¾" (14.3 cm)

⅝" (1.5 cm) of the miter

¼" (0.7 cm)

Opening to turn right side out

Top

A

⅝" (1.5 cm) of the miter

¾" (2 cm)

2" (5 cm)

6" (15 cm)

Fold the center of the bottom

9 ¾" (25 cm)

*Sew using a ¼" (0.7 cm) seam allowance, unless otherwise noted.

Full-Size Template

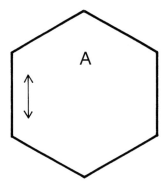

A

Sew the makeup case.

1

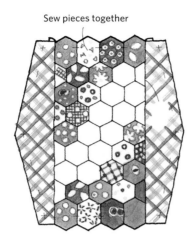

Sew pieces together

1. Make the case top: Sew the hexagon pieces together into nine rows. Sew the rows together until all hexagon pieces are sewn together, as shown in the above diagram. Trim the case top. With right sides together, sew a top piece to each long side of the case top. Next, fold bag with wrong sides together and trim, as shown in the patchwork diagram on page 48.

2

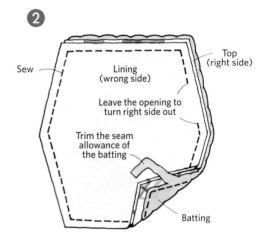

Sew · Top (right side) · Lining (wrong side) · Leave the opening to turn right side out · Trim the seam allowance of the batting · Batting

2. Press the fusible batting to wrong side of the case top. With right sides together, layer the top and lining and sew along edges. Leave an opening.

3

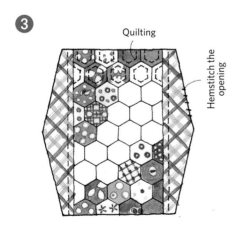

Quilting · Hemstitch the opening

3. Turn case right side out and quilt, as shown in the patchwork diagram on page 48. Hemstitch opening closed.

4

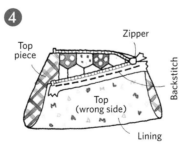

Top piece · Zipper · Backstitch · Top (wrong side) · Lining

4. Attach zipper to case top by backstitching ⅛" (0.3 cm) from the raw edge of the zipper.

5

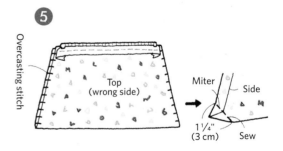

Overcasting stitch · Top (wrong side) · Miter · Side · 1¼" (3 cm) · Sew

5. Fold the case and sew side seams using an overcast stitch. Miter corners by stitching across each corner at 1¼" (3 cm), as shown in the above diagram. Add charms to the zipper pull to finish the case.

Log Cabin

Constructed from simple rectangles and artfully arranged, log cabin blocks are great for "building" little gifts. Easy piecing techniques help you master the traditional log cabin block and courthouse steps variation in these vibrant projects:

Pin Cushions

Placemat

Slouchy Shoulder Bag

Rectangular Pillow

Table Topper

Quilted Tote Bag

Square Throw Pillows

13 Pin Cushions

Play with the arrangement of your fabrics to shape unique variations of the classic log cabin block. Frame a favorite image, follow a color scheme, or pick a completely random arrangement—the choice is yours in these pin cushions.

Materials

Red & White Pin Cushion
Assorted red prints
1½" x 21¾" (3.5 x 55 cm) in total
Assorted white prints
1½" x 15¾" (3.5 x 40 cm) in total

Multi-Colored Pin Cushion
Assorted prints
2¾" x 17¾" (7 x 45 cm) in total

Orange & Purple Pin Cushion
Assorted purple prints
1½" x 21¾" (3.5 x 55 cm) in total
Assorted orange prints
1½" x 15¾" (3.5 x 40 cm) in total

Pig Pin Cushion
Green print
1½" x 1½" (4 x 4 cm)
Pink print
1½" x 9¾" (3.5 x 25 cm)
Blue print
1½" x 11¾" (3.5 x 30 cm)
Yellow print
1½" x 15¾" (3.5 x 40 cm)

For All Pin Cushions
Backing
8" x 8" (20.5 x 20.5 cm)
Batting
6" x 6" (15 x 15 cm)
Stuffing
Cotton pillow stuffing

Cut the fabric.

Trace and cut out templates **A-M** on page 53 (following template cutting instructions on page 107). Cut fabric pieces adding a ¼" (0.7 cm) seam allowance:

Red & White Pin Cushion (Diagram A)
• 1 each: **A, D, E, H, I, L, M** of red prints = 7 total pieces
• 1 each: **B, C, F, G, J, K** of white prints = 6 total pieces

Multi-Colored Pin Cushion (Diagram A)
• 1 each: **A-M** of assorted prints = 13 total pieces

Orange & Purple Pin Cushion (Diagram A)
• 1 each: **A, D, E, H, I, L, M** of purple prints = 7 total pieces
• 1 each: **B, C, F, G, J, K** of orange prints = 6 total pieces

Pig Pin Cushion (Diagram B)
• 1 **A** piece of green print
• 1 each: **B-E** of pink print = 4 total pieces
• 1 each: **F-I** of blue print = 4 total pieces
• 1 each: **J-M** of yellow print = 4 total pieces

For All Pin Cushions
• 2 backing pieces:
3½" x 3½" (9 x 9 cm)

*Sew using a ¼" (0.7 cm) seam allowance, unless otherwise noted.

Patchwork Diagram A

Top

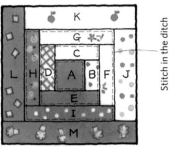

Stitch in the ditch

3½" (9 cm)

Patchwork Diagram B

Top

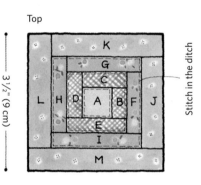

3½" (9 cm)

3½" (9 cm)

Stitch in the ditch

Backing

Center

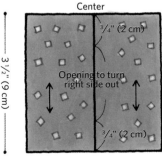

¾" (2 cm)

Opening to turn right side out

¾" (2 cm)

3½" (9 cm)

3½" (9 cm)

Sew the pin cushion.

1

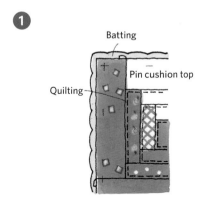

Batting
Pin cushion top
Quilting

2

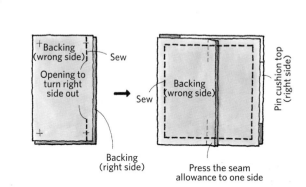

+Backing (wrong side)
Sew
Opening to turn right side out
Backing (right side)
Sew
Backing (wrong side)
Pin cushion top (right side)
Press the seam allowance to one side

1. Make the pin cushion top: Sew the pieces together into a log cabin block. With wrong sides together, layer the log cabin block, batting, and one backing piece. Baste and quilt, as shown in the above diagram.

2. Cut remaining backing piece in half, then sew the center back seam, leaving an opening to turn right side out. With right sides together, layer backing and pin cushion top and sew along the edges.

3

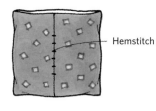

Turn right side out
Stuff with cotton
Hemstitch

3. Turn right side out and fill with stuffing. Hemstitch opening to complete the pin cushion.

Full-Size Templates

*Begin at starting point and measure to end of each letter for full-size templates.

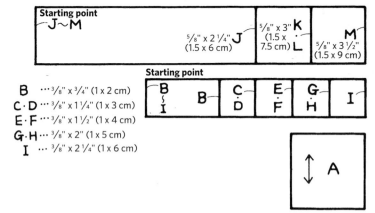

Starting point
J~M

$5/8$" x $2 1/4$" J (1.5 x 6 cm)
$5/8$" x 3" K (1.5 x 7.5 cm) L
M $5/8$" x $3 1/2$" (1.5 x 9 cm)

B ··· $3/8$" x $3/4$" (1 x 2 cm)
C·D ··· $3/8$" x $1 1/4$" (1 x 3 cm)
E·F ··· $3/8$" x $1 1/2$" (1 x 4 cm)
G·H ··· $3/8$" x 2" (1 x 5 cm)
I ··· $3/8$" x $2 1/4$" (1 x 6 cm)

Starting point
B I B C D E F G H I

A

14 Placemat

This placemat features six log cabin blocks, each in the same design but with different orientation. It doubles as a basket cover, a decorative wall hanging, or anything else you can imagine.

Materials

Dark color prints
7 ³⁄₄" x 29 ½" (20 x 75 cm)

White eyelet fabric
6" x 39 ¼" (15 x 100 cm)

Batting 13 ³⁄₄" x 17 ³⁄₄" (35 x 45 cm)

Backing 13 ³⁄₄" x 17 ³⁄₄" (35 x 45 cm)

Binding (pink polka dot print)
11 ³⁄₄" x 11 ³⁄₄" (30 x 30 cm)

Patches
Six ³⁄₄" (2 cm) lace flower patches

Buttons
Six ⅛" (3 mm) buttons

Patchwork Diagram

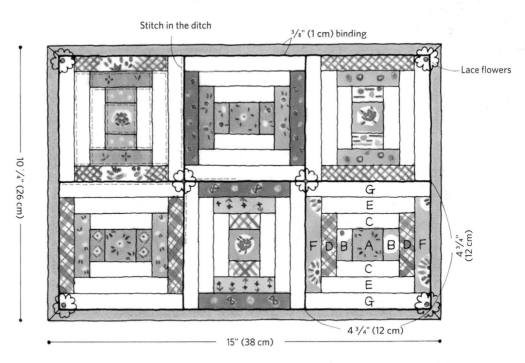

Stitch in the ditch

³⁄₈" (1 cm) binding

Lace flowers

10 ¼" (26 cm)

4 ³⁄₄" (12 cm)

4 ³⁄₄" (12 cm)

15" (38 cm)

G E C F D B A B D F C E G

How to Attach the Beads

Beads

Lace flowers

*Sew using a ¼" (0.7 cm) seam allowance, unless otherwise noted.

Cut the fabric.

Trace and cut out templates **A-G** below (following template cutting instructions on page 107). Cut fabric pieces adding a ¼" (0.7 cm) seam allowance:

- 6 **A** pieces of dark color prints
- 12 each: **B**, **D**, **F** of dark color prints = 36 total pieces
- 12 each: **C**, **E**, **G** of white eyelet fabric = 36 total pieces
- Binding: Make a 1½" (4 cm)-wide and 55" (140 cm)-long binding by sewing bias strips together. Refer to page 125.

Sew the quilt.

1. Make the quilt top: Sew the pieces together into six courthouse steps blocks. Refer to patchwork diagram on page 55 for placement of dark and light fabrics.

2. With wrong sides together, layer the quilt top, batting, and backing. Baste and quilt, as shown in the patchwork diagram on page 55.

3. Sew the binding to the quilt, following binding instructions on pages 124-127.

4. Attach the lace flowers and beads, as shown in the patchwork diagram on page 55.

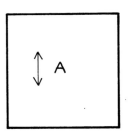

Full-Size Templates

*Begin at starting point and measure to end of each letter for full-size templates.

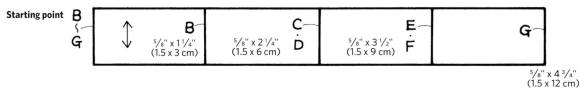

15 Slouchy Shoulder Bag

Courthouse step blocks create this distinctive shoulder bag. Opt for a solid background if you want the log cabin blocks to stand out.

Materials

Fabric a (dark denim)
23 1/2" x 43 1/4" (60 x 110 cm)

Fabric b (light denim)
17 3/4" x 19 3/4" (45 x 50 cm)

Fabric c (brown checkered print)
7 3/4" x 21 3/4" (20 x 55 cm)

Fabric d (orange print)
4" x 43 1/4" (10 x 110 cm)

Fusible batting
19 3/4" x 35 1/2" (50 x 90 cm)

Fusible Interfacing (lightweight)
7 3/4" x 27 1/2" (20 x 70 cm)

Lining (beige print)
19 3/4" x 37 1/2" (50 x 95 cm)

Loops
Two metal loops
(1 1/2" [4 cm] in diameter)

Button
One magnetic button
(5/8" [1.5 cm] in diameter)

Patchwork Diagram

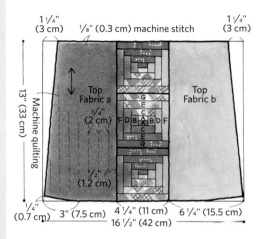

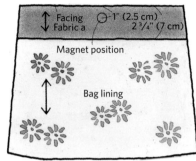

Cut the fabric.

Trace and cut out templates **A-G** on page 60 (following template cutting instructions on page 107). Cut fabric pieces adding a 1/4" (0.7 cm) seam allowance:

- 6 each: **B**, **D**, **F** of fabric a = 18 total pieces
- 6 each: **B**, **D**, **F** of fabric b = 18 total pieces
- 6 each: **A**, **C**, **E**, **G** of fabric c = 24 total pieces
- 6 each: **A**, **C**, **E**, **G** of fabric d = 24 total pieces
- 2 top pieces of fabric a

- 2 top pieces of fabric b
- 1 bottom piece of fabric c
- 1 bottom lining
- 2 facing pieces of fabric a
- 2 lining pieces
- 1 handle piece of fabric a, cut without seam allowance: 3 1/2" x 37" (9 x 94 cm)
- 1 handle piece of fabric c, cut without seam allowance: 2 1/4" x 37" (6 x 94 cm)

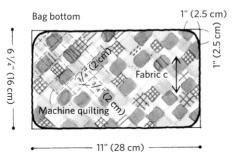

Bag bottom

1" (2.5 cm)

1" (2.5 cm)

6 1/4" (16 cm)

Fabric c

3/4" (2 cm)

3/4" (2 cm)

Machine quilting

11" (28 cm)

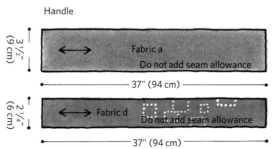

Handle

3 1/2" (9 cm)

Fabric a
Do not add seam allowance

37" (94 cm)

2 1/4" (6 cm)

Fabric d
Do not add seam allowance

37" (94 cm)

*Sew using a 1/4" (0.7 cm) seam allowance, unless otherwise noted.

Sew the bag.

1

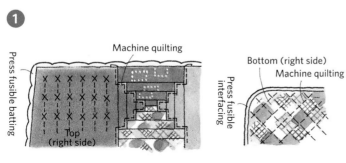

Press fusible batting

Machine quilting

Top (right side)

Press fusible interfacing

Bottom (right side)
Machine quilting

2

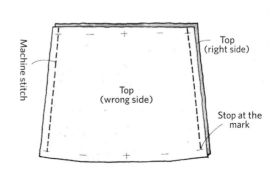

Machine stitch

Top (right side)

Top (wrong side)

Stop at the mark

1. Make the bag top: Sew the pieces together into three courthouse steps blocks. Sew the blocks together. With right sides together, sew a top piece to each long side of the blocks. Press the fusible batting to wrong side of the bag top. Quilt, as shown in the above diagram. Repeat this step to make the other side of the bag. Make the bag bottom by pressing the fusible interfacing to wrong side of the bottom piece and quilt.

2. With right sides together, sew the bag sides. Stop at the mark, approximately 1/4" (0.7 cm) from the bottom. Press seams open.

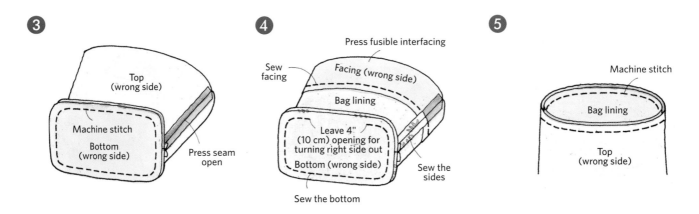

3 With right sides together, sew the bag bottom to the bag.

4. Make the bag lining: Press fusible interfacing to wrong side of facing pieces. Sew the facing and bag lining pieces with right sides together. Next, with right sides together, sew the lining side seams. Stop ¼" (0.7 cm) from the bottom as in step 2. Press seams open. Sew the bottom lining to the bag lining. Leave an opening to turn right side out.

5. With right sides together, insert the lining into the bag and sew the opening edge closed.

Full-Size Templates

*Begin at starting point and measure to end of each letter for full-size templates.

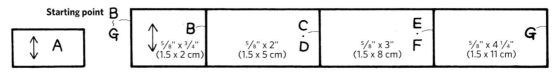

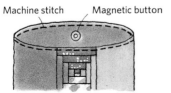

Machine stitch   Magnetic button

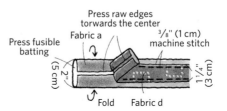

Press raw edges
torwards the center

Press fusible
batting

Fabric a

³/₈" (1 cm)
machine stitch

2"
(5 cm)

1¼"
(3 cm)

Fold   Fabric d

6. Turn the bag right side out through the opening in the lining. Hemstitch the opening closed. Attach magnetic button pieces to the lining at the center of the bag on each side.

7. Make the handle: Press fusible batting to wrong side of the handle piece of fabric a. Fold and align the two handle pieces of fabrics a and d. Topstitch down each side of the handle piece of fabric d, using a ³/₈" (1 cm) seam allowance. Cut two 9" (23 cm) pieces from the handle to make the tabs.

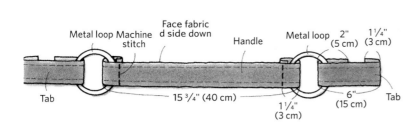

Metal loop Machine
stitch

Face fabric
d side down

Handle

Metal loop   2"
(5 cm)

1¼"
(3 cm)

Tab

15 ³/₄" (40 cm)

1¼"
(3 cm)

6"
(15 cm)

Tab

Handle

Tab

1¼" (3 cm)

⁵/₈" (1.5 cm)

1¼" (3 cm)

1¼" (3 cm)

³/₄" (2 cm)

Side

8. Thread the handle and tabs through the metal loops. Secure the handle by folding each end over and stitching near the metal loops.

9. Attach a tab to each side of the bag by stitching as shown in the above diagram.

16 Rectangular Pillow

This long, sturdy pillow showcases the log cabin block in its simplest form and adds a playful twist with fun fabrics. Finish with big herringbone quilting stitches for more unique detail.

Materials

Assorted prints
   Apple print 3" x 5" (8 x 13 cm)
   Stripe print 3" x 5" (8 x 13 cm)
   Assorted red prints
   5 ½" x 27 ½" (14 x 70 cm)
   Assorted blue prints
   6" x 23 ½" (15 x 60 cm)

Batting
11 ¾" x 17 ¾" (30 x 45 cm)

Pillow top backing (muslin)
11 ¾" x 17 ¾" (30 x 45 cm)

Backing 11 ¾" x 23 ½" (30 x 60 cm)

Thread
6-strand embroidery floss (red)

Pillow Form
10" x 16" (25.5 x 41 cm) pillow form

Patchwork Diagram

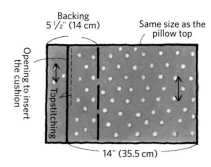

Herringbone stitch (use 2 strands red floss)

E

C

F   D   B   A   B   D   F

C

E

10 ¼" (26 cm)

16" (41 cm)

4 ¼" (11 cm)

2 ⅛" (5.5 cm)

6 ¼" (16 cm)

8 ½" (21 cm)

2" (5 cm)

2" (5 cm)

12" (31 cm)

2" (5 cm)

2" (5 cm)

2 ¼" (6 cm)

*Sew using a ¼" (0.7 cm) seam allowance, unless otherwise noted.

Backing
5 ½" (14 cm)

Same size as the
pillow top

Opening to insert
the cushion

Topstitching

14" (35.5 cm)

Cut the fabric.

Create templates using measurements noted below for pieces **A-F**. Cut fabric pieces from assorted prints adding a ¼" (0.7 cm) seam allowance:

• 1 **A** piece of apple print:
   2 ¼" x 4 ¼" (6 x 11 cm)
• 2 **B** pieces of stripe print:
   2 ⅛" x 2 ¼" (5.5 x 6 cm)
• 2 **C** pieces (1 each of assorted red prints and assorted blue prints):
   2" x 8 ½" (5 x 21 cm)

• 2 **D** pieces (1 each of assorted red prints and assorted blue prints):
   2" x 6 ¼" (5 x 16 cm)
• 2 **E** pieces (1 each of assorted red prints and assorted blue prints):
   2" x 12" (5 x 31 cm)
• 2 **F** pieces (1 each of assorted red prints and assorted blue prints):
   2" x 10 ¼" (5 x 26 cm)
• 1 backing piece: 5 ½" x 10 ¼" (14 x 26 cm)
• 1 backing piece:
   10 ¼" x 14" (26 x 35.5 cm)

Sew the pillow.

①

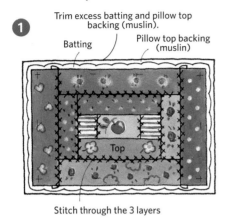

Trim excess batting and pillow top backing (muslin).

Batting

Pillow top backing (muslin)

Top

Stitch through the 3 layers

②

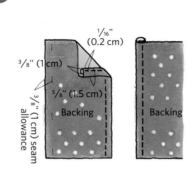

$^1/_{16}$" (0.2 cm)

$^3/_8$" (1 cm)

$^5/_8$" (1.5 cm)

$^3/_8$" (1 cm) seam allowance

Backing

Backing

③

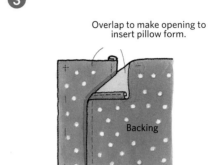

Overlap to make opening to insert pillow form.

Backing

Basting

1. Make the pillow top: Sew pieces **A-F** together into a log cabin block. With wrong sides together, layer the log cabin block, batting, and pillow top backing (muslin). Quilt with the herringbone stitch, as shown in the above diagram.

2. Hem the backing pieces by folding fabric $^3/_8$" (1 cm) to wrong side, then folding again $^5/_8$" (1.5 cm) and topstitching at $^1/_{16}$" (0.2 cm).

3. Overlap the two backing pieces to equal the same size as the pillow top and baste along the top and bottom at overlap.

④

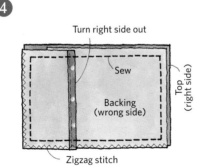

Turn right side out

Sew

Backing (wrong side)

Top (right side)

Zigzag stitch

4. With right sides together, align pillow top and backing and sew around all four sides. Zigzag stitch seam allowances. Turn pillow right side out through opening. Insert pillow form to finish.

Herringbone stitch

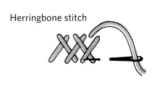

17 Table Topper

With its burst of color at the center, this design show-cases the versatility of log cabin squares and adds liveliness to any table.

Materials

Assorted prints
  Flower print
  4 ³/₄" x 4 ³/₄" (12 x 12 cm)
  Assorted orange prints
  6 ¹/₄" x 31 ¹/₂" (16 x 80 cm)
  Assorted white prints
  6 ¹/₄" x 27 ¹/₂" (16 x 70 cm)

Batting
15 ³/₄" x 15 ³/₄" (40 x 40 cm)

Backing
15 ³/₄" x 15 ³/₄" (40 x 40 cm)

Binding (orange checkered print)
11 ³/₄" x 11 ³/₄" (30 x 30 cm)

Patchwork Diagram

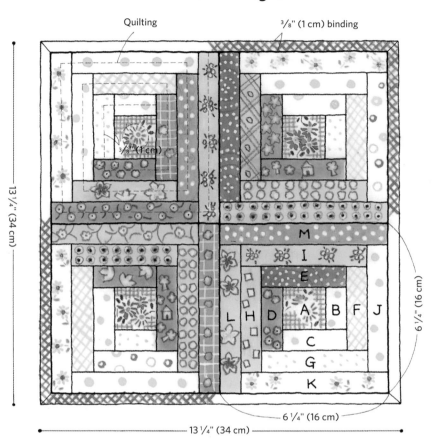

*Sew using a ¹/₄" (0.7 cm) seam allowance, unless otherwise noted.

Cut the fabric.

Trace and cut out templates **A-M** below (following template cutting instructions on page 107). Cut fabric pieces adding a ¼" (0.7 cm) seam allowance:

- 4 **A** pieces of flower print
- 4 each: **D**, **E**, **H**, **I**, **L**, **M** of assorted orange prints = 24 total pieces
- 4 each: **B**, **C**, **F**, **G**, **J**, **K** of assorted white prints = 24 total pieces
- Make a 1½" (4 cm)-wide and 59" (150 cm)-long binding by sewing bias strips together. Refer to page 125.

Sew the quilt.

1. Make the quilt top: Sew the pieces together into four log cabin blocks. Sew the four blocks together, as shown in the patchwork diagram on page 66.

2. With wrong sides together, layer the quilt top, batting, and backing. Quilt, as shown in the patchwork diagram on page 66.

3. Sew the binding to the quilt, following binding instructions on pages 124-127.

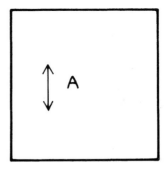

Full-Size Templates

*Begin at starting point and measure to end of each letter for full-size templates.

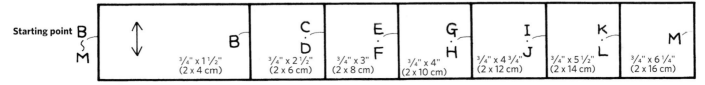

Starting point

| B | | | | | | |
| M | | | | | | |

	B	C / D	E / F	G / H	I / J	K / L	M
		¾" x 1½" (2 x 4 cm)	¾" x 2½" (2 x 6 cm)	¾" x 3" (2 x 8 cm)	¾" x 4" (2 x 10 cm)	¾" x 4¾" (2 x 12 cm)	¾" x 5½" (2 x 14 cm)	¾" x 6¼" (2 x 16 cm)

18 Quilted Tote Bag

Two log cabin blocks are paired side by side and finished with hand-stitched details in this roomy bag.

Materials

Assorted prints
7 ¾" x 43 ¼" (20 x 110 cm) in total

Main fabric (beige)
15 ¾" x 31 ½" (40 x 80 cm)

Edge fabric (pink)
9 ¾" x 15 ¾" (25 x 40 cm)

Batting
15 ¾" x 31 ½" (40 x 80 cm)

Lining 15 ¾" x 31 ½" (40 x 80 cm)

Decorative fabric a (dark pink)
4" x 7 ¾" (10 x 20 cm)

Decorative fabric b (brown)
4" x 7 ¾" (10 x 20 cm)

Buttons
Four wrapped buttons
(1 ½" [4 cm] in diameter)
One set of magnetic buttons
(⅜" [1 cm] in diameter)

Handles
One set of handles
(17 ¾" [45 cm]-long)

Thread
6-strand embroidery floss
(red, beige, brown)

Rick rack
5 ¾" (40 cm) of ¼" (6 mm)-wide
rick rack

Patchwork Diagram

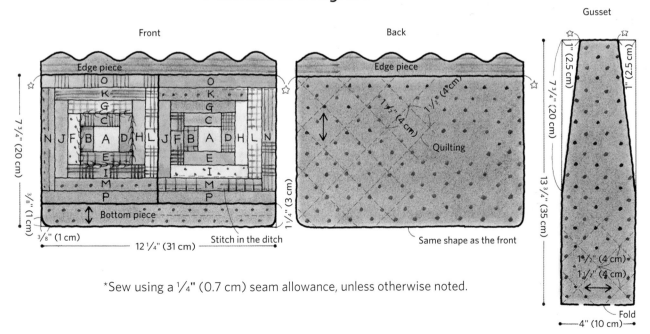

*Sew using a ¼" (0.7 cm) seam allowance, unless otherwise noted.

Cut the fabric.

Trace and cut out templates **A-P** on page 72 (following template cutting instructions on page 107). Cut fabric pieces adding a ¼" (0.7 cm) seam allowance:

- 2 each: **A-P** of assorted prints = 32 total pieces
- 1 bottom piece of main fabric: 1¼" x 12¼" (3 x 31 cm)
- 1 backing piece of main fabric: 7¾" x 12¼" (20 x 31 cm)
- 2 lining pieces: 7¾" x 12¼" (20 x 31 cm)
- 1 gusset piece of main fabric
- 1 gusset lining piece
- 4 edge pieces of edge fabric
- 4 circles of decorative fabric a: 3" (8 cm) in diameter
- 4 circles of decorative fabric b: 1½" (4 cm) in diameter

Sew the bag.

❶

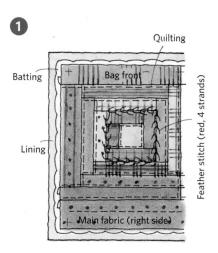

❷

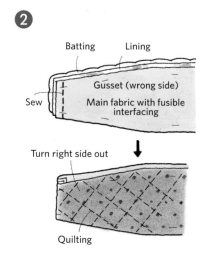

❸

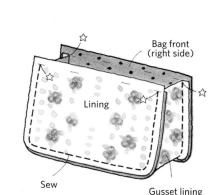

1. Make the bag front: Sew the pieces together into two log cabin blocks. Sew the two blocks together and attach the bottom piece. With wrong sides together, layer the bag front, batting, and one lining piece. Quilt and embroider, as shown above.

2. Press fusible interfacing to wrong side of gusset. With right sides together, layer the gusset, lining, and batting and sew along the short edges. Turn right side out and quilt, as shown in the above diagram.

3. With wrong sides together, layer the bag back, batting, and lining. Quilt, as shown in the patchwork diagram on page 69. With right sides together, align the bag back with the gusset at star marks and sew along the edges, using a ⅜" (1 cm) seam allowance. Repeat with the bag front.

4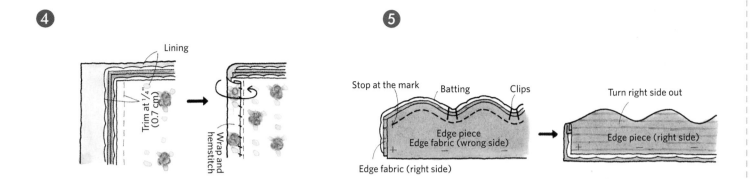

Lining

Trim at ¼" (0.7 cm)

Wrap and hemstitch

5

Stop at the mark   Batting   Clips

Edge piece
Edge fabric (wrong side)

Edge fabric (right side)

Turn right side out

Edge piece (right side)

4. For each gusset seam allowance, trim the batting, main fabric, and top layer of the lining to ¼" (0.7 cm), leaving the bottom layer of the lining uncut. Fold the bottom layer of the lining, wrap it around the ¼" (0.7 cm) seam allowance, and hemstitch.

5. With right sides together, layer two edge pieces and batting and stitch along the curved edge. Turn right side out. Repeat for other edge piece.

6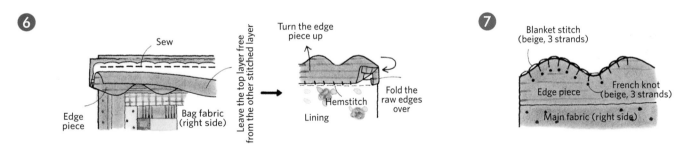

Sew

Edge piece

Bag fabric (right side)

Leave the top layer free from the other stitched layer

Turn the edge piece up

Hemstitch

Lining

Fold the raw edges over

7

Blanket stitch (beige, 3 strands)

Edge piece

French knot (beige, 3 strands)

Main fabric (right side)

6. With right sides together, sew one edge piece to the bag front, leaving the top layer of the edge piece free. Turn the edge piece up and press. Turn the edge piece seam allowance under and fold the raw edges over. Hemstitch edge piece to lining. Repeat with other edge piece and bag back.

7. Blanket stitch along the curve of the edge pieces. Next, stitch French knots.

8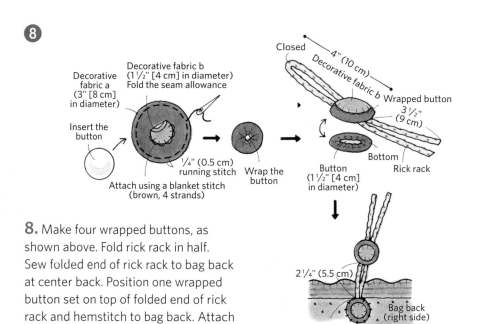

Decorative fabric a (3" [8 cm] in diameter)

Decorative fabric b (1 ½" [4 cm] in diameter) Fold the seam allowance

Insert the button

Attach using a blanket stitch (brown, 4 strands)

¼" (0.5 cm) running stitch

Wrap the button

Button (1 ½" [4 cm] in diameter)

Closed

4" (10 cm)

Decorative fabric b

Wrapped button 3 ½" (9 cm)

Bottom

Rick rack

2 ¼" (5.5 cm)

Bag back (right side)

Insert the closed side of the rick rack between the button and the bag, then hemstitch.

8. Make four wrapped buttons, as shown above. Fold rick rack in half. Sew folded end of rick rack to bag back at center back. Position one wrapped button set on top of folded end of rick rack and hemstitch to bag back. Attach other wrapped button set to rick rack, as shown above.

9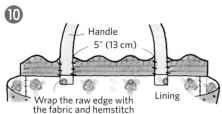

Attach the magnet

⅝" (1.7 cm)

Bottom side

Bag front (right side)

9. Sew the magnets to the bag front and the back of the wrapped button.

10

Handle 5" (13 cm)

Wrap the raw edge with the fabric and hemstitch

Lining

10. Sew the handles to the bag, using a hemstitch, to finish.

Full-Size Templates

*Begin at starting point and measure to end of each letter for full-size templates.

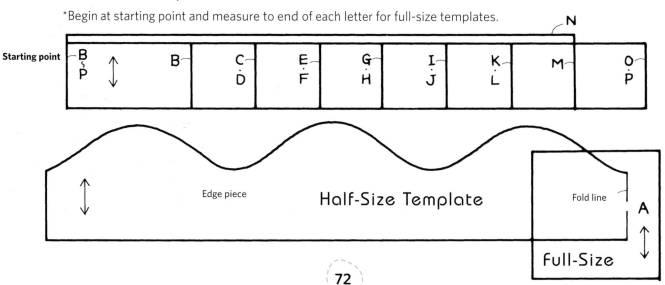

Starting point

N

B P | B | C D | E F | G H | I J | K L | M | O P

Edge piece

Half-Size Template

Fold line

A

Full-Size

19 Square Throw Pillows

These square pillows turn simple log cabin blocks into dynamic, colorful designs. Stitch up these coordinating accessories to add a cozy, homey touch to any room!

Materials

Assorted prints
  Red print 2" x 6" (5 x 15 cm)
  Assorted green or blue prints
  7 ³⁄₄" x 31 ¹⁄₂" (20 x 80 cm)
  Assorted pink or brown prints
  7 ³⁄₄" x 35 ¹⁄₂" (20 x 90 cm)

Batting 17 ³⁄₄" x 17 ³⁄₄" (45 x 45 cm)

Pillow top backing (cotton muslin
foundation)
17 ³⁄₄" x 17 ³⁄₄" (45 x 45 cm)

Backing (checkered print)
17 ³⁄₄" x 23 ¹⁄₂" (45 x 60 cm)

Pillow form
16" x 16" (41 x 41 cm) pillow form

Cut the fabric.

Trace and cut out templates **A-M** on
page 75 (following template cutting
instructions on page 107). Cut fabric
pieces adding a ¹⁄₄" (0.7 cm) seam
allowance:

- 4 **A** pieces of red print
- 4 each: **B**, **C**, **F**, **G**, **J**, **K** of assorted green
  prints or blue prints = 24 total pieces
- 4 each: **D**, **E**, **H**, **I**, **L**, **M** of assorted pink
  prints or brown prints = 24 total pieces
- 1 backing piece: 2 ³⁄₄" x 16" (7 x 41 cm)
- 1 backing piece:
  5 ¹⁄₂" x 16" (6 x 41 cm)

Patchwork Diagram

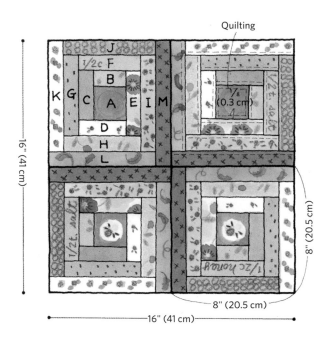

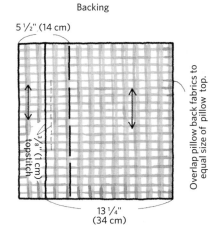

Backing

*Sew using a ¹⁄₄" (0.7 cm) seam allowance, unless otherwise noted.

Sew the pillow.

1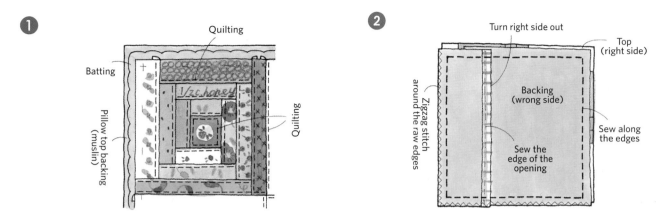

Quilting

Batting

Pillow top backing (muslin)

Quilting

1/2c honey

2

Turn right side out

Top (right side)

Zigzag stitch around the raw edges

Backing (wrong side)

Sew the edge of the opening

Sew along the edges

1. Make the pillow top: Sew pieces **A-M** together into four log cabin blocks. Sew the four log cabin blocks together. Layer the pillow top, batting, and pillow top backing (muslin) together and quilt, as shown in the above diagram.

2. Follow instructions on page 64 to sew the backing pieces. With right sides together, align the pillow top and backing and sew around all four sides. Zigzag stitch seam allowances. Turn pillow right side out through opening. Insert pillow form to finish.

Full-Size Templates

*Begin at starting point and measure to end of each letter for full-size template

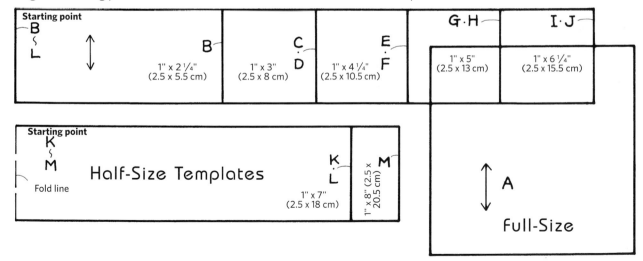

Starting point
B
C
L

↕

B
1" x 2 ¼"
(2.5 x 5.5 cm)

C
D
1" x 3"
(2.5 x 8 cm)

E
F
1" x 4 ¼"
(2.5 x 10.5 cm)

G·H

I·J

1" x 5"
(2.5 x 13 cm)

1" x 6 ¼"
(2.5 x 15.5 cm)

Starting point
K
L
M

Fold line

Half-Size Templates

K
L
1" x 7"
(2.5 x 18 cm)

M
1" x 8" (2.5 x 20.5 cm)

↕

A

Full-Size

Stars & Polygons

The stars and shapes in these projects build on your square-sided sewing foundation. You can use these basic piecing techniques for creating unique shapes, including pinwheels and six-pointed stars. See these design elements at work in these projects:

Quilted Tray

Pinwheel Quilts

Round Zippered Pouches

House Basket

Makeup Case

Sweet Home Potholders

21 Quilted Tray

A simple six-pointed patchwork star anchors the bottom of this small hexagonal tray. This piece is perfect for corralling all your loose sewing essentials.

Materials

Assorted prints
9 ¾" x 9 ¾"(25 x 25 cm)

Solid white 9 ¾" x 9 ¾" (25 x 25 cm)

Top and backing fabric (small yellow flower print)
19 ¾" x 23 ½" (50 x 60 cm)

Batting 11 ¾" x 21 ¾" (30 x 55 cm)

Cut the fabric.

Trace and cut out templates **A** and **B** below (following template cutting instructions on page 107). Cut fabric pieces adding a ¼" (0.7 cm) seam allowance:

• 6 **A** pieces of assorted prints
• 6 **A** pieces of solid white
• 12 **B** pieces of top fabric
• 6 **B** pieces of batting

Patchwork Diagram

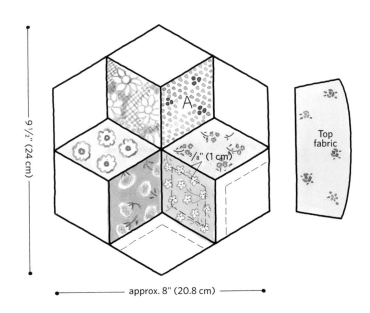

*Sew using a ¼" (0.7 cm) seam allowance, unless otherwise noted.

Full-Size Templates

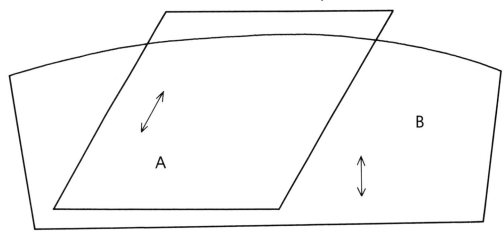

Sew the tray.

❶

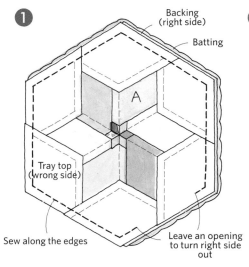

Backing (right side)

Batting

A

Tray top (wrong side)

Sew along the edges

Leave an opening to turn right side out

1. Make the tray top: Sew the pieces together, as shown in the above diagram. With right sides together, layer the tray top, backing, and batting and sew along the edges. Leave an opening on one side.

❷

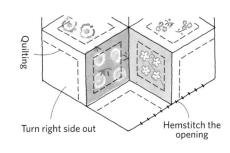

Batting

Trim the seam allowance of the batting

2. Trim the seam allowance of the batting.

❸

Quilting

Turn right side out

Hemstitch the opening

3. Turn right side out and hemstitch the opening closed. Quilt, as shown in the above diagram.

❹

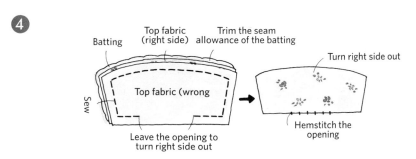

Batting

Top fabric (right side)

Trim the seam allowance of the batting

Turn right side out

Top fabric (wrong

Sew

Leave the opening to turn right side out

Hemstitch the opening

4. Make the side pieces: With right sides together, layer the top fabric, backing, and batting and sew along the edges. Leave an opening. Turn right side out and hemstitch the opening closed. Repeat this step until all six side pieces are complete.

❺

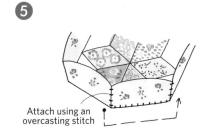

Attach using an overcasting stitch

5. Attach the sides to the tray using an overcasting stitch.

20 Pinwheel Quilts

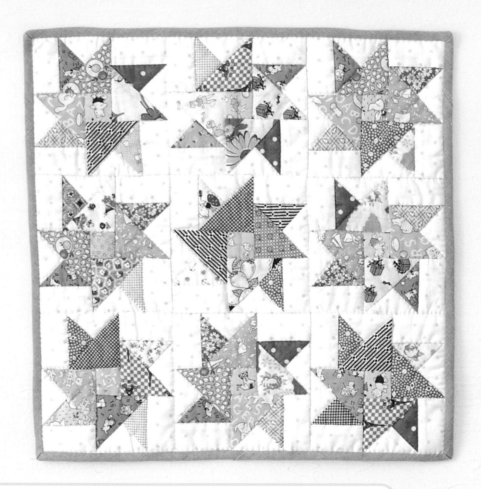

Displayed on a wall, draped over the back of a chair, or set atop a table, these mini quilts are colorful, cute, and versatile. Their clean lines and classic pinwheel design can be personalized to your décor.

Materials (pinwheel quilt #1)

Assorted prints
21 ³⁄₄" x 23 ¹⁄₂" (55 x 60 cm) in total

Background fabric
19 ³⁄₄" x 21 ³⁄₄" (50 x 55 cm)

Batting
21 ³⁄₄" x 21 ³⁄₄" (55 x 55 cm)

Backing (print)
21 ³⁄₄" x 21 ³⁄₄" (55 x 55 cm)

Binding (solid brown)
15 ³⁄₄" x 15 ³⁄₄" (40 x 40 cm)

Cut the fabric.

Trace and cut out templates **A-D** on page 83 (following template cutting instructions on page 107). Cut fabric pieces adding a ¹⁄₄" (0.7 cm) seam allowance:

- 36 **A** pieces of assorted prints
- 72 **B** pieces of assorted prints
- 36 **C** pieces of assorted prints
- 9 **D** pieces of assorted prints
- Binding: Make a 1 ¹⁄₂" (4cm)-wide and 78 ³⁄₄" (2 m)-long binding by sewing bias strips together. Refer to page 125.

Patchwork Diagram

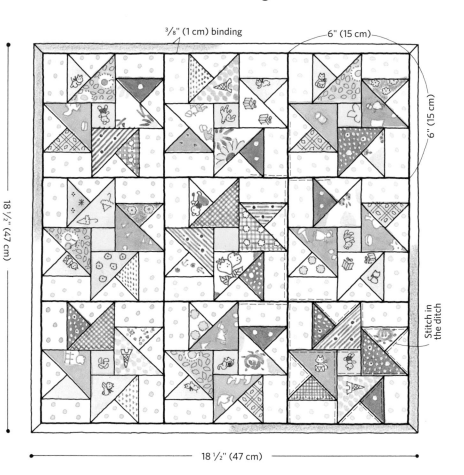

³⁄₈" (1 cm) binding

6" (15 cm)

6" (15 cm)

18 ¹⁄₂" (47 cm)

Stitch in the ditch

18 ¹⁄₂" (47 cm)

*Sew using a ¹⁄₄" (0.7 cm) seam allowance, unless otherwise noted.

Sew the block.

1. Make nine star blocks by sewing pieces **A-D** together, as shown in the below diagram.

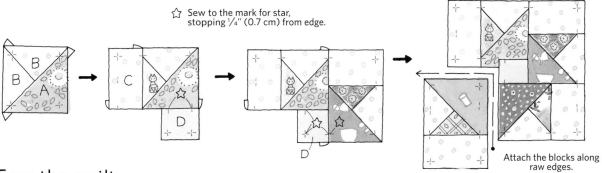

☆ Sew to the mark for star, stopping ¼" (0.7 cm) from edge.

Attach the blocks along raw edges.

Sew the quilt.

1. Make the quilt top: Sew the blocks together into rows of three blocks each. Sew the rows together to complete the quilt top.

2. With wrong sides together, layer the quilt top, batting, and backing. Quilt, as shown in the patchwork diagram on page 82.

3. Sew the binding to the quilt, following binding instructions on pages 124-127.

Full-Size Templates

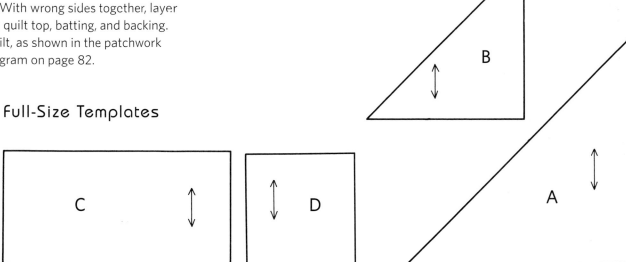

Materials (pinwheel quilt #2)

Assorted prints
19 3/4" x 27 3/4" (50 x 70 cm) in total

Background fabric
15 3/4" x 21 3/4" (40 x 55 cm)

Batting
21 3/4" x 21 3/4" (55 x 55 cm)

Backing (print)
21 3/4" x 21 3/4" (55 x 55 cm)

Binding (solid brown)
15 3/4" x 15 3/4" (40 x 40 cm)

Cut the fabric.

Trace and cut out templates **A-G** on page 85 (following template cutting instructions on page 107). Cut fabric pieces adding a 1/4" (0.7 cm) seam allowance:

- 40 **A** pieces of assorted prints
- 20 **B** pieces of assorted prints
- 20 **C** pieces of assorted prints
- 32 **D** pieces of assorted prints
- 16 **E** pieces of assorted prints
- 16 **F** pieces of assorted prints
- 4 **G** pieces of assorted prints
- Binding: Make a 1 1/2" (4cm)-wide and 78 3/4" (2 m)-long binding by sewing bias strips together. Refer to page 125.

Patchwork Diagram

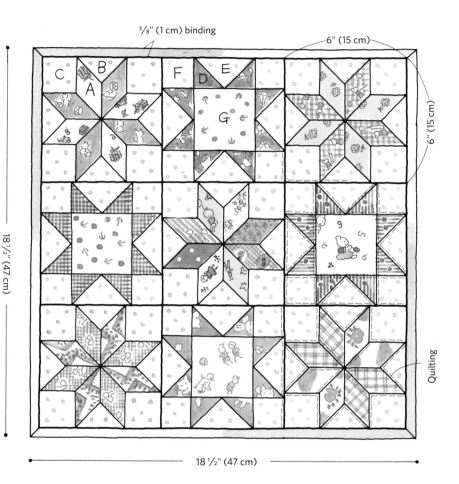

3/8" (1 cm) binding

6" (15 cm)

6" (15 cm)

18 1/2" (47 cm)

Quilting

18 1/2" (47 cm)

*Sew using a 1/4" (0.7 cm) seam allowance, unless otherwise noted.

Sew the quilt.

1. Make the two types of star blocks: Sew the pieces together as shown in the diagrams to the right. Make nine star blocks total. Make the quilt top by sewing alternating blocks together into rows of three blocks each. Sew the rows together to complete the quilt top, as shown in the patchwork diagram on page 84.

2. With wrong sides together, layer the quilt top, batting, and backing. Quilt, as shown in the patchwork diagram on page 84.

3. Sew the binding to the quilt, following binding instructions on pages 124-127.

Sew Block #1

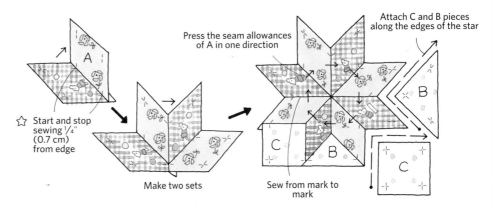

Press the seam allowances of A in one direction

Attach C and B pieces along the edges of the star

☆ Start and stop sewing ¼" (0.7 cm) from edge

Make two sets

Sew from mark to mark

Sew Block #2

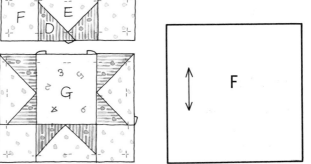

Full-Size Templates

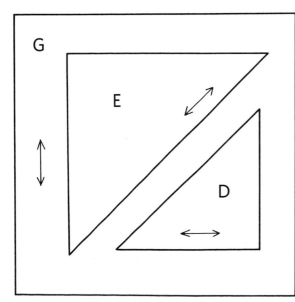

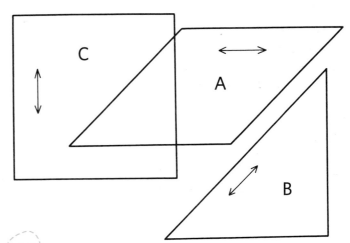

85

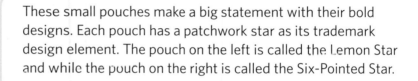

These small pouches make a big statement with their bold designs. Each pouch has a patchwork star as its trademark design element. The pouch on the left is called the Lemon Star and while the pouch on the right is called the Six-Pointed Star.

Materials (lemon star pouch)

Fabric a (navy flower print) 4" x 6" (10 x 15 cm)

Fabric b (purple checkered) 6" x 7 ³⁄₄" (15 x 20 cm)

Fabric c (blue stripe) 4" x 6" (10 x 15 cm)

Top, bottom, and binding (green checkered)
17 ³⁄₄" x 19 ³⁄₄" (45 x 50 cm)

Batting 7" x 13 ³⁄₄" (18 x 35 cm)

Lining (purple checkered) 7" x 13 ³⁄₄" (18 x 35 cm)

Zipper
One 7" (18 cm)–long zipper

Materials (six-pointed star pouch)

Fabric a (fruit print) 4" x 7 ³⁄₄" (10 x 20 cm)

Fabric b (red checkered) 6" x 7 ³⁄₄" (15 x 20 cm)

Fabric c (small white flower print)
6"x 9 ³⁄₄" (15 x 25 cm)

Binding (small red flower print)
13 ³⁄₄" x 15 ³⁄₄" (35 x 40 cm)

Batting 7" x 13 ³⁄₄" (18 x 35 cm)

Lining (small white flower print) 7" x 13 ³⁄₄" (18 x 35 cm)

Zipper
One 7" (18 cm)–long zipper

Cut the fabric.

Trace and cut out templates **A** and **B** on page 90 (following template cutting instructions on page 107). Cut fabric pieces adding a ¹⁄₄" (0.7 cm) seam allowance:

• 6 **A** pieces of fabric a
• 12 **A** pieces of fabric b
• 6 **A** pieces of fabric c
• 6 **B** pieces of top fabric
• 2 lining pieces: 5 ¹⁄₄" (13.4 cm) in diameter
• 1 bottom piece: 5 ¹⁄₄" (13.4 cm) in diameter
• Binding: Make a 1 ¹⁄₂" (4cm)-wide and 19 ³⁄₄" (50 cm)-long binding by sewing bias strips together. Refer to page 125.

Cut the fabric.

Trace and cut out templates **A–C** on page 90 (following template cutting instructions on page 107). Cut fabric pieces adding a ¹⁄₄" (0.7 cm) seam allowance:

• 2 **A** pieces of fabric a
• 12 **B** pieces of fabric b
• 12 **C** pieces of fabric c
• 2 lining pieces: 5 ¹⁄₄" (13.4 cm) in diameter
• Binding: Make a 1 ¹⁄₂" (4cm)-wide and 19 ³⁄₄" (50 cm)-long binding by sewing bias strips together. Refer to page 125.

Patchwork Diagram

Six-Pointed Star Pouch

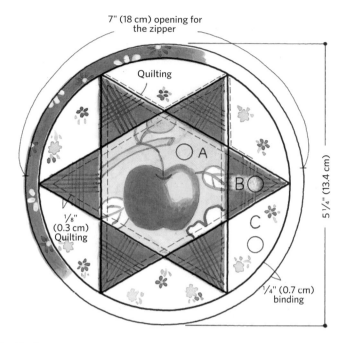

7" (18 cm) opening for the zipper

Quilting

O A
B O
C O

1/8" (0.3 cm) Quilting

1/4" (0.7 cm) binding

5 1/4" (13.4 cm)

*Sew using a 1/4" (0.7 cm) seam allowance, unless otherwise noted.

Lemon Star Pouch

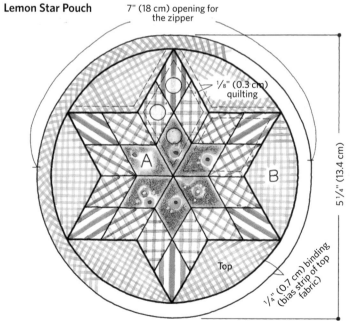

7" (18 cm) opening for the zipper

1/8" (0.3 cm) quilting

A

B

Top

1/4" (0.7 cm) binding (bias strip of top fabric)

5 1/4" (13.4 cm)

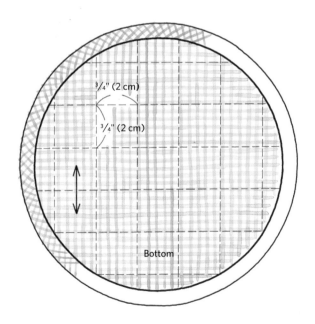

3/4" (2 cm)

3/4" (2 cm)

Bottom

Sew the pouch.

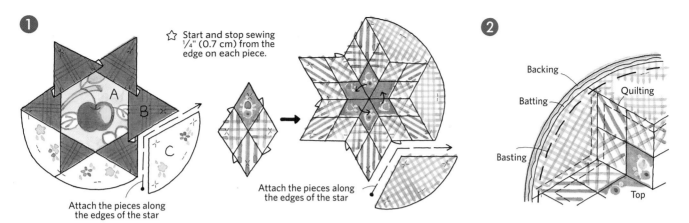

①

☆ Start and stop sewing ¼" (0.7 cm) from the edge on each piece.

Attach the pieces along the edges of the star

Attach the pieces along the edges of the star

②

Backing

Batting

Basting

Quilting

Top

1. For each pouch, make the top by sewing the pieces together, as shown in the above diagrams. Start and stop sewing ¼" (0.7 cm) from the edge on each piece. For the Six-Pointed Star Pouch, make two star blocks (one for each side).

2. With wrong sides together, layer the top, batting, and lining and baste around the edge. Quilt, as shown in the above diagram. Repeat step for the pouch bottom.

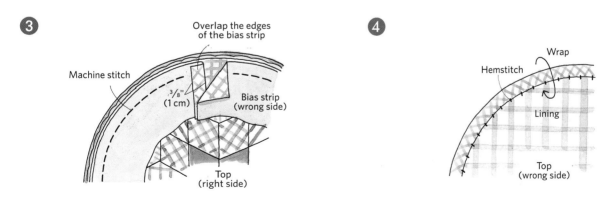

③

Overlap the edges of the bias strip

Machine stitch

⅜" (1 cm)

Bias strip (wrong side)

Top (right side)

④

Wrap

Hemstitch

Lining

Top (wrong side)

3. Sew the binding around each pouch piece.

4. Wrap the binding around the seam allowance and hemstitch the binding to the lining.

5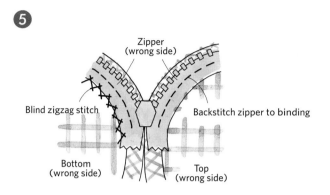

Zipper (wrong side)

Blind zigzag stitch

Backstitch zipper to binding

Bottom (wrong side)

Top (wrong side)

6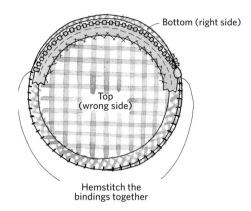

Bottom (right side)

Top (wrong side)

Hemstitch the bindings together

5. Attach zipper to each side of the opening edge, by backstitching through the inside layer of the binding only. Blind zigzag stitch the raw edge of the zipper to the lining.

6. With right sides together, align the pouch top and bottom and hemstitch the bindings together to finish the pouch.

Full-Size Templates

Six-Pointed Star Pouch

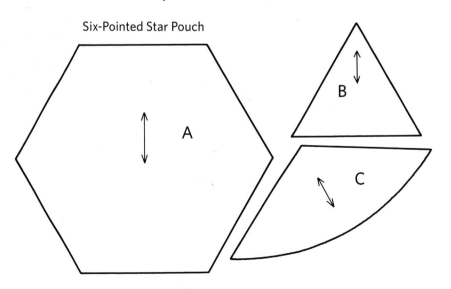

A

B

C

Lemon Star Pouch

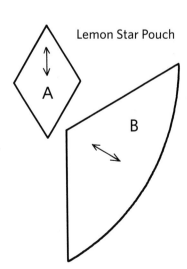

A

B

23 House Basket

This basket makes an adorable home for all of your odds and ends. Polygons are pieced together into house blocks and attached to a square bottom to build a beautiful and functional basket.

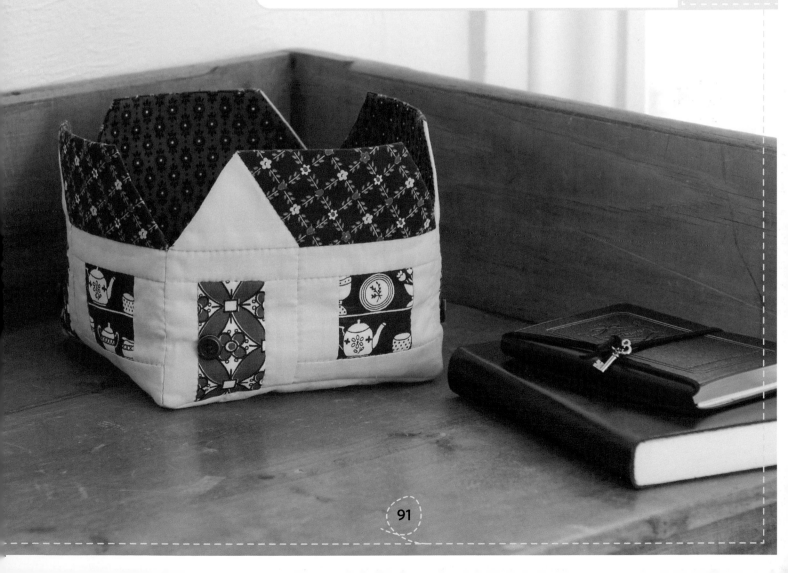

Materials

Fabric a (yellow print)
15 ¾" x 21 ¾" (40 x 55 cm)

Fabric b (flower print)
4" x 8" (10 x 20 cm)

Fabric c (black flower print)
6" x 11 ¾" (15 x 30 cm)

Fabric d (brown dish print)
6" x 6" (15 x 15 cm)

Lining (red print)
11 ¾" x 21 ¾" (30 x 55 cm)

Fusible batting
11 ¾" x 21 ¾" (30 x 55 cm)

Buttons
Four ⅜" (1 cm) buttons

Patchwork Diagram

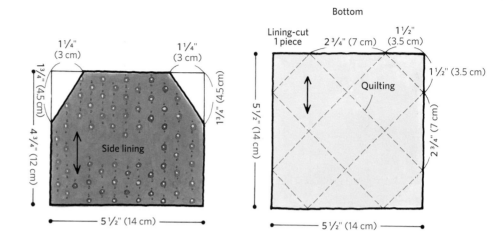

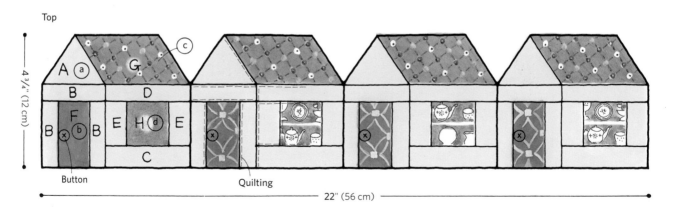

*Sew using a ¼" (0.7 cm) seam allowance, unless otherwise noted.

Cut the fabric.

Trace and cut out templates **A-H** on page 94 (following template cutting instructions on page 107). Cut fabric pieces adding a ¼" (0.7 cm) seam allowance:

- 4 **A** pieces of fabric a
- 12 **B** pieces of fabric a
- 4 **C** pieces of fabric a
- 4 **D** pieces of fabric a
- 8 **E** pieces of fabric a
- 4 **F** pieces of fabric b
- 4 **G** pieces of fabric c
- 4 **H** pieces of fabric d
- 1 bottom piece of fabric a
- 4 side lining pieces
- 1 bottom lining piece

Sew the basket.

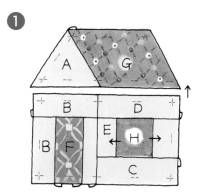

1. Make the basket top: Sew pieces **A-H** together into the house block, as shown in the diagram to the left. Make four blocks.

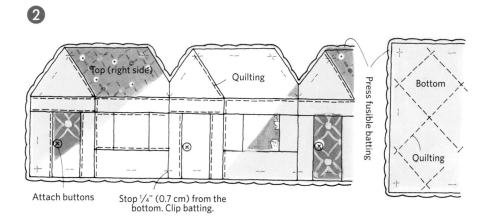

2. Sew the four blocks together, stopping ¼" (0.7 cm) from the bottom on each seam. Press the fusible batting to wrong side of the blocks. Make clips and trim excess. Press the fusible batting to wrong side of bottom piece. Quilt, as shown in the above diagram.

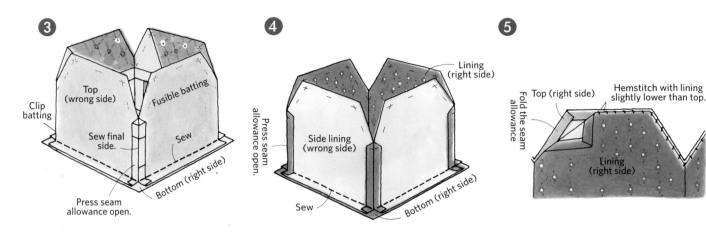

3 Clip batting · Top (wrong side) · Fusible batting · Sew final side. · Sew · Press seam allowance open. · Bottom (right side)

4 Press seam allowance open. · Lining (right side) · Side lining (wrong side) · Sew · Bottom (right side)

5 Fold the seam allowance · Top (right side) · Hemstitch with lining slightly lower than top. · Lining (right side)

3. Sew the final side of the blocks together. Press the seam allowance open. With right sides together, sew blocks to the bottom piece along each side.

4. Sew the lining sides and bottom together following the same process as step 3.

5. With wrong sides together, insert the lining into the basket top. Fold over the seam allowance on both pieces and hemstitch together.

Full-Size Templates

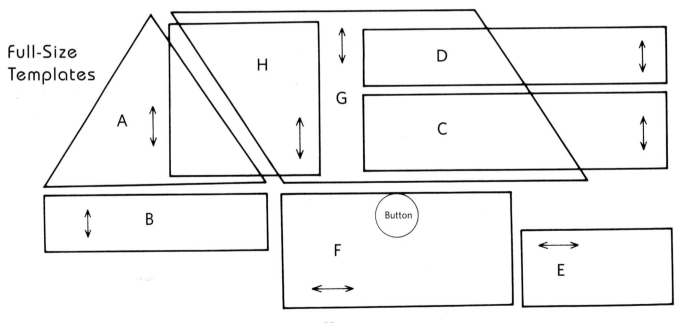

A · H · B · G · D · C · F · Button · E

24 Makeup Case

This small pouch sports a retro color combination, but you can choose any fabric you like—anything goes. The simple, elegant patchwork pattern in this design is called the Evening Star.

Materials

Fabric a (yellow print)
11 ³⁄₄" x 11 ³⁄₄"(30 x 30 cm)

Fabric b (red polka dot)
6" x 13 ³⁄₄" (15 x 35 cm)

Fabric c (gray flower)
4" x 6" (10 x 15 cm)

Bottom fabric (red flower)
13 ³⁄₄"x 15 ³⁄₄" (35 x 40 cm)

Fusible batting
9 ³⁄₄" x 9 ³⁄₄" (25 x 25 cm)

Lining (white print)
7 ³⁄₄" x 7 ³⁄₄" (20 x 20 cm)

Zipper
One 6 ³⁄₄" (17 cm)-long zipper

Patchwork Diagram

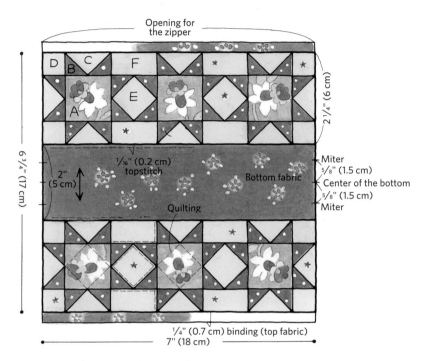

*Sew using a ¹⁄₄" (0.7 cm) seam allowance, unless otherwise noted.

Cut the fabric.

Trace and cut out templates **A–F** on page 98 (following template cutting instructions on page 107). Cut fabric pieces adding a ¹⁄₄" (0.7 cm) seam allowance:

• 6 **A** pieces of fabric c
• 48 **B** pieces of fabric b
• 16 **C** pieces of fabric a

• 8 **D** pieces of fabric a
• 4 **E** pieces of fabric a
• 8 **F** pieces of fabric a
• 1 bottom piece
• Binding: Make a 1 ¹⁄₂" (4cm)-wide and 17 ³⁄₄" (45 cm)-long binding by sewing bias strips together. Refer to page 125.

Sew the makeup case.

❶

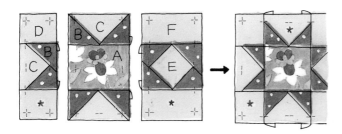

1. Make the case top: Sew pieces **A-F** together into six star blocks, as shown in the above diagram. Make two sets of three blocks each. With right sides together, sew one set to each long edge of the case bottom.

❷

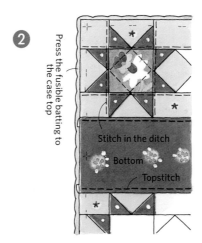

Press the fusible batting to the case top

Stitch in the ditch

Bottom

Topstitch

2. Press the fusible batting to wrong side of case top and quilt, as shown in the above diagram.

❸

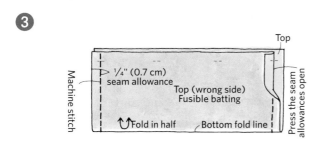

Machine stitch

Top

¼" (0.7 cm) seam allowance

Top (wrong side) Fusible batting

↑ Fold in half   Bottom fold line

Press the seam allowances open

3. With right sides together, fold the case top in half and sew the sides. Press seam allowances open.

❹

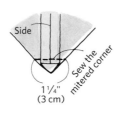

Side

Sew the mitered corner

1¼" (3 cm)

4. Sew the mitered corners: Fold the outside bottom corners with right sides together to make a triangle. Stitch ³⁄₈" (1 cm) from triangle point. Turn right side out. Repeat steps 3 and 4 for the case lining. With wrong sides together, insert lining into the case.

Full-Size Templates

⑤

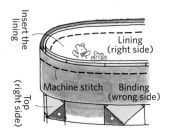 

Insert the lining

Lining (right side)

Wrap and hemstitch

Top (right side)

Machine stitch   Binding (wrong side)

5. Sew the binding to the top opening edge. Wrap the binding around the seam allowance and hemstitch binding to the lining.

⑥

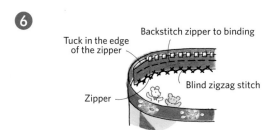

Tuck in the edge of the zipper

Backstitch zipper to binding

Blind zigzag stitch

Zipper

6. Attach zipper to each side of the opening edge, by backstitching through the inside layer of the binding only. Blind zigzag stitch the raw edge of the zipper to the lining.

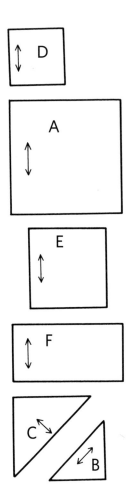

D

A

E

F

C   B

25 Sweet Home Potholders

These quirky and colorful potholders will brighten your day. Polygons are pieced together to construct the houses in these fun patchwork blocks.

Materials (for potholder on left)

Assorted prints
   fabric a (light blue small flower print)
   6" x 7 ¾" (15 x 20 cm)
   fabric b (yellow polka dot) 6" x 7 ¾" (15 x 20 cm)
   fabric c (red stripe) 6" x 6" (15 x 15 cm)
   fabric d (girl print) 3" x 3" (8 x 8 cm)
   fabric e (black heart print) 3" x 4" (8 x 10 cm)
   fabric f (red flower print) 2 ¼" x 7 ¾" (6 x 20 cm)

Batting 7 ¾" x 15 ¾" (20 x 40 cm)

Backing (small red flower print)
7¾" x 7 ¾" (20 x 20 cm)

Binding (checkered) 19 ¾" x 21 ¾" (50 x 55 cm)

Button
One button (¼" [0.7 cm] in diameter)

Materials (for potholder on right)

Assorted prints:
   fabric a (brown checkered) 7 ¾" x 11 ¾" (20 x 30 cm)
   fabric b (blue flower print) 4" x 7 ¾" (10 x 20 cm)
   fabric c (yellow stripe) 4" x 7 ¾" (10 x 20 cm)
   fabric d (plain red) 3" x 4" (8 x 10 cm)
   fabric e (dish print) 3" x 6" (8 x 15 cm)
   fabric f (orange print) 2 ¼" x 7 ¾" (6 x 20 cm)

Batting 7 ¾" x 15 ¾" (20 x 40 cm)

Backing
7 ¾" x 7 ¾" (20 x 20 cm)

Binding (print) 19 ¾" x 21 ¾" (50 x 55 cm)

Button
One button (¼" [0.7 cm] in diameter)

Cut the fabric.

Trace and cut out templates **A–K** on page 103 (following template cutting instructions on page 107). Cut fabric pieces adding a ¼" (0.7 cm) seam allowance:

- 3 **A** pieces of fabric a
- 1 **B** piece of fabric a
- 1 **B'** piece of fabric a
- 1 **C** piece of fabric b
- 2 **D** pieces of fabric b
- 2 **E** pieces of fabric b
- 1 **F** piece of fabric b
- 1 **G** piece of fabric c
- 2 **H** pieces of fabric c
- 1 **I** piece of fabric e

- 1 **J** piece of fabric d
- 1 **K** piece of fabric f
- 1 tab piece, cut without seam allowance: 1 ½" x 4" (4 x 10 cm)
- Make a 1 ½" (4 cm)-wide and 15 ¾" (40 cm)-long binding by sewing bias strips together. Refer to page 125.

Cut the fabric.

Trace and cut out templates **A–J** on page 104 (following template cutting instructions on page 107). Cut fabric pieces adding a ¼" (0.7 cm) seam allowance:

- 2 **A** pieces of fabric a
- 1 **B** piece of fabric a
- 1 **B'** piece of fabric a
- 2 **C** pieces of fabric a
- 2 **D** pieces of fabric c
- 2 **E** pieces of fabric c
- 1 **F** piece of fabric b
- 1 **G** piece of fabric b
- 1 **H** piece of fabric d
- 2 **I** pieces of fabric e

- 1 **J** piece of fabric f
- 1 tab piece, cut without seam allowance: 1 ½" x 4" (4 x 10 cm)
- Make a 1 ½" (4 cm)-wide and 15 ¾" (40 cm)-long binding by sewing bias strips together. Refer to page 125.

Patchwork Diagram

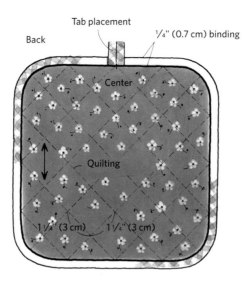

Back

Tab placement

Center

¼" (0.7 cm) binding

Quilting

1¼" (3 cm)   1¼" (3 cm)

*Sew using a ¼" (0.7 cm) seam allowance, unless otherwise noted.

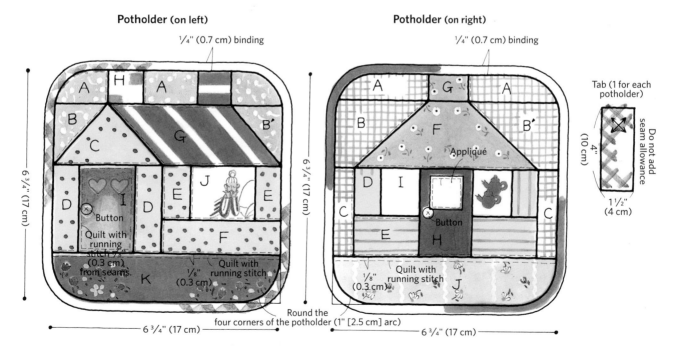

Potholder (on left)

¼" (0.7 cm) binding

A H A

B   B'

C

G

D I D E J E

Button

Quilt with running stitch ⅛" (0.3 cm) from seams.

F

Quilt with running stitch ⅛" (0.3 cm)

K

6¾" (17 cm)

6¾" (17 cm)

Potholder (on right)

¼" (0.7 cm) binding

A G A

B   B'

F

Appliqué

D I

C   C

E H

Button

⅛" (0.3 cm)

Quilt with running stitch

J

6¾" (17 cm)

6¾" (17 cm)

Round the four corners of the potholder (1" [2.5 cm] arc)

Tab (1 for each potholder)

Do not add seam allowance

4" (10 cm)

1½" (4 cm)

101

Sew the potholders.

1

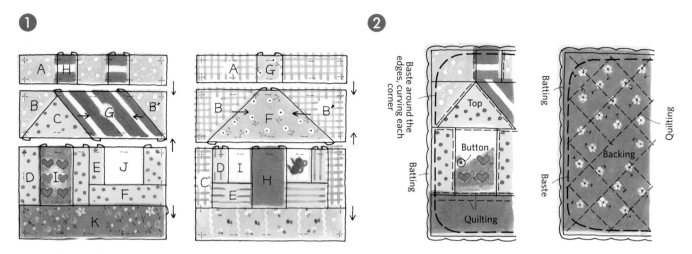

1. Make the potholder top: Sew pieces **A-K** together into the house block, as shown in the above diagram.

2

2. Layer the potholder top and batting. Baste and quilt, as shown in the above diagram. Layer the backing and batting. Baste and quilt, as shown in the above diagram.

3

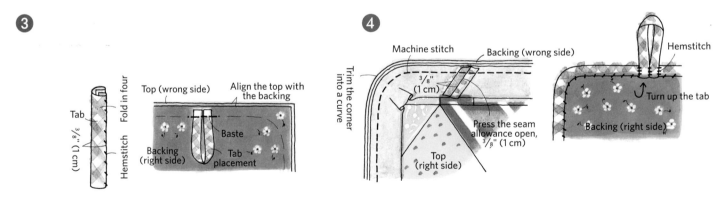

3. Make the tab: Fold the tab piece and hemstitch the long edge. Baste the tab to the potholder backing, as shown in the above diagram.

4

4. With wrong sides together, align the potholder top and backing. Sew on the binding. Wrap binding around the seam allowance and hemstitch. Turn tab up and hemstitch to binding to complete the potholder.

Full-Size Templates
Potholder (on left)

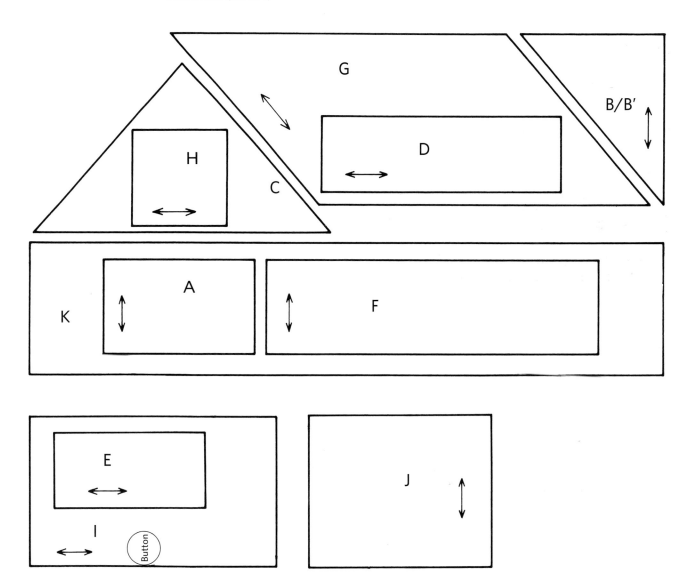

Full-Size Templates
Potholder (on right)

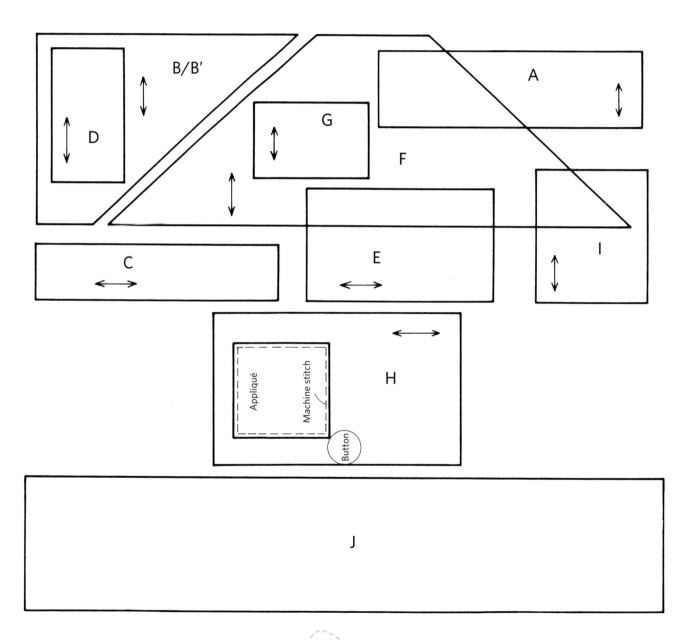

Patchwork
Tools & Techniques

Tools

Ruler

Pencils: Use pencils with softer lead, such as 2B, to draw lines on patterns and fabrics.

Paper scissors:
Use to cut patterns.

Thread for piecework and quilting: Opt for a cotton/polyester blend.

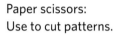

Thread scissors

Fabric scissors

Quilting pins

Basting thread

Thimbles: When quilting, the leather thimble is used to push the needle and the metal thimble is used to receive the needle tip.

Quilting hoop: At 11 ¾" (30cm) in diameter, this tool is useful for quilting larger projects.

Quilting needle

Patchwork needle

Basting needle

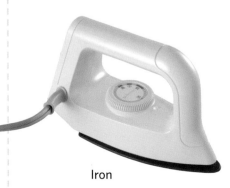

Iron

Bias tape maker: Insert the bias strips through the opening and press with the iron to make binding strips.

Basic Patchwork Techniques

How to make a pattern template and cut the fabric.

1. For each project, trace patterns for the pieces directly onto paper or cardboard using a ruler. Next, cut out along the drawn lines to create the template.

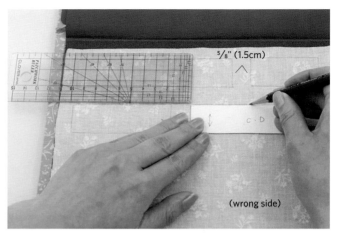

⁵⁄₈" (1.5cm)

(wrong side)

2. Using a pencil with a soft lead (such as 2B), trace pattern templates onto the wrong side of the fabric. Leave a ⁵⁄₈" (1.5 cm) space between pieces.

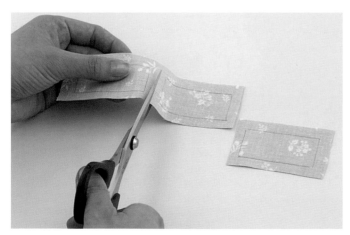

3. Cut the pieces with a ¼" (0.7 cm) seam allowance.

4. After cutting, lay out the pieces into the quilt design. This visual review ensures all the needed pieces have been cut.

Square Patchwork Techniques

How to make a four-patch block.

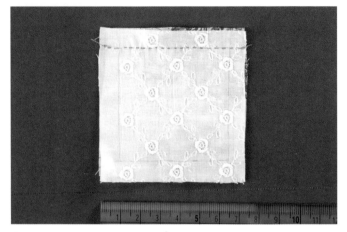

1. Sew from edge to edge. Make two sets.

2. Press the seam allowances toward the print fabric.

3. Attach the two sets by sewing from edge to edge. Press the center seam allowance to one side.

4. Front view of completed four-patch block.

Hexagon Patchwork Techniques

How to make a hexagon flower.

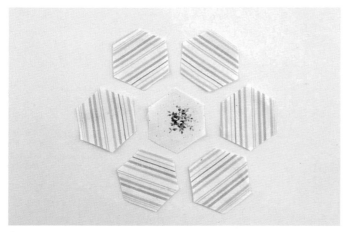

1. After cutting, lay out all the pieces according to the hexagon flower design.

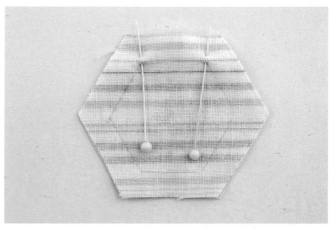

2. Align the center piece with one petal piece.

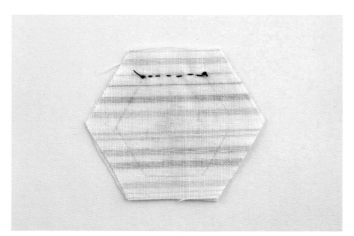

3. Sew along the seam line, starting and stopping ¼" (0.7 cm) from each edge.

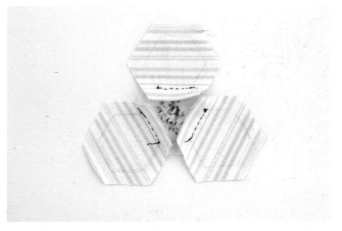

4. With right sides together, sew three petal pieces to three sides of the center piece.

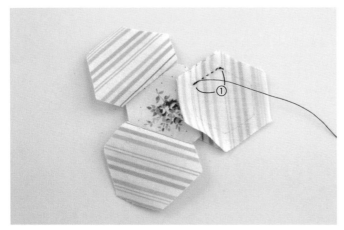

5. With right sides together, align side ① of two petal pieces and sew along the seam line, starting and stopping ¼" (0.7 cm) from each edge.

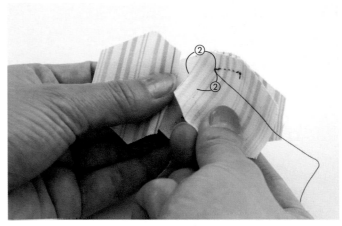

6. With right sides together, align side ② of the petal piece with side ② of the center piece and sew along the seam line, starting and stopping ¼" (0.7 cm) from each edge.

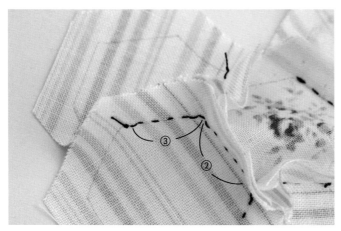

7. With right sides together, align side ③ of two petal pieces and sew along the seam line, starting and stopping ¼" (0.7 cm) from each edge.

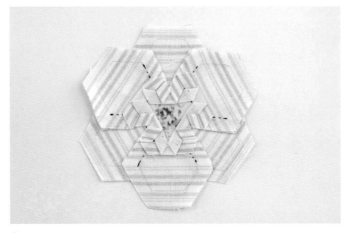

8. Continue attaching the remaining three petal pieces as shown in previous steps. Press three of the center seam allowances open.

How to sew the outer petals.

For the petal fabric

Vertical   Horizontal

By changing the direction of the petal fabric print, you can change the appearance of the flower patchwork block.

1. Sew 12 outer petals in groups of three, as shown in the picture.

Front

Back

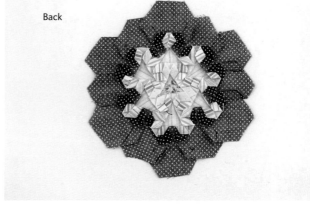

2. Attach outer petals to the flower. Press the center seam allowances open.

How to make hexagon rows.

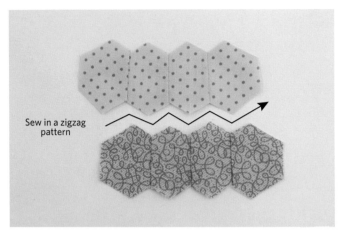

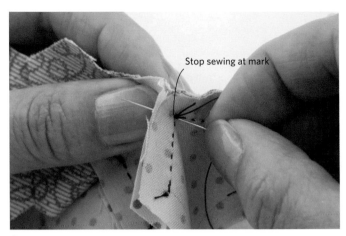

Stop sewing at mark

1. When the pieces are not flower shaped, it is quick and easy to sew them together in rows. Sew along seam line in a zigzag pattern, starting and stopping ¼" (0.7 cm) from each edge.

2. Sew the rows together, piece by piece, starting and stopping ¼" (0.7 cm) from each edge.

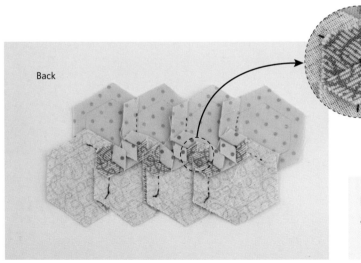

Back

3. Press the seam allowances open.

Pressing seam allowances open reduces unwanted bulk and creates a neater finished design.

How to use the English paper piecing method.

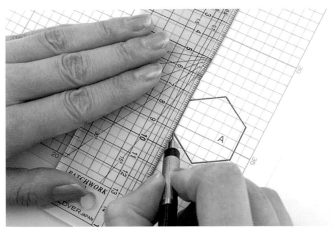

1. In this technique, you will use a paper pattern template for each hexagon piece. Create a paper template for each fabric piece in the design.

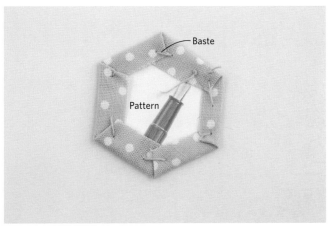

2. Place the paper pattern template on the wrong side of the fabric. Fold the seam allowance around the paper and baste through the pattern template inside. Repeat process for all pieces.

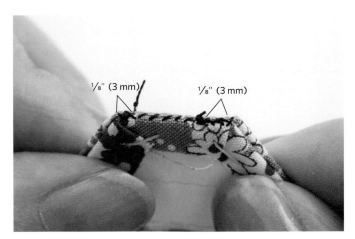

3. Align two pieces and insert needle ⅛" (3 mm) in from right corner. Whipstitch to right corner, then change direction of stitching and sew to left corner. At left corner, bring the needle back ⅛" (3 mm), make a knot and cut the thread.

4. When you sew the center piece on, sew one side using a whipstitch.

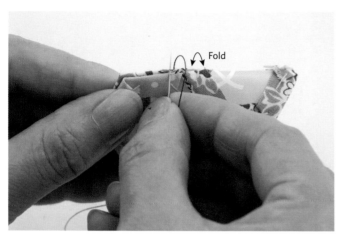

5. With right sides together, align the center piece with the next petal piece, and sew using a whipstitch. Fold the petals as needed to bring edges together as you sew.

6. After sewing all the pieces, remove the basting stitches and pattern templates.

7. Press the seam allowances.

In hexagonal patchwork, the English paper piecing method is used to sew the pieces together using paper templates and a whipstitch. This technique is ideal for beginners since the seam allowance opens easily.

Log Cabin Patchwork Techniques

How to make a log cabin block.

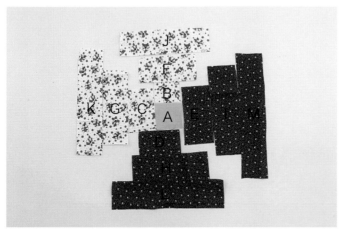

1. After cutting, lay out all the pieces according to the log cabin block design. For the log cabin block design, start sewing from the center towards the outside in a spiral pattern.

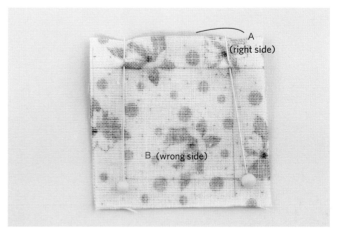

2. With right sides together, align central pieces A and B.

3. Start sewing from the edge by making a single backstitch.

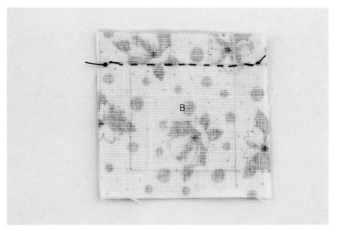

4. Sew to the edge and make a single backstitch to end seam.

5. Open the block and press the seam allowance towards the outside piece using your finger.

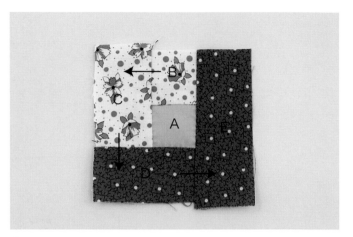

6. Continue attaching pieces, working from the inside of the block toward the outside, shown above in alphabetical order. Press the seam allowances in the directions indicated by arrows.

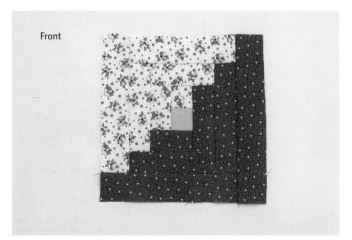

Front

Back

7. Completed log cabin block. Press using the iron.

How to make a courthouse steps block.

1. After cutting, lay out all the pieces according to the courthouse steps design. For courthouse steps design, start sewing from the center, then continue in the following order: left, right, top, and bottom.

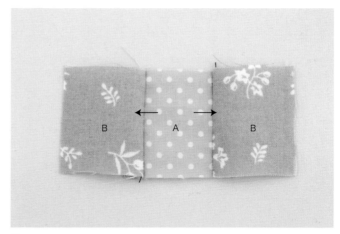

2. Align central pieces A and B and sew from edge to edge. Press the seam allowances toward the outside B pieces.

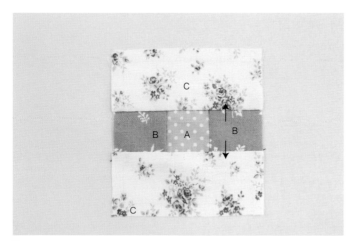

3. Sew C pieces to the block. Press the seam allowances in the directions indicated by arrows.

4. Continue attaching pieces in alphabetical order to complete the courthouse steps block. Press using the iron.

Star & Polygon Patchwork Techniques

How to make a star block.

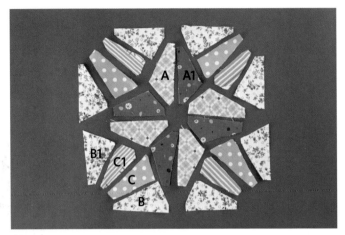

1. After cutting, lay out all the pieces according to the star design.

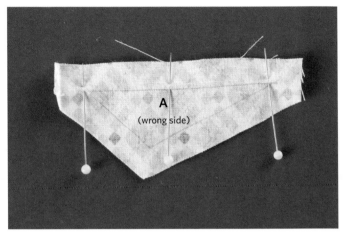

2. With right sides together, align piece A with A1 and insert pins at both sides and at center.

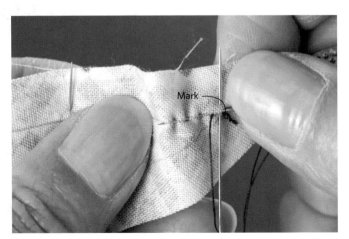

3. Starting ¼" (0.7 cm) from the edge, make a single backstitch.

4. Sew along the seam line, stopping ¼" (0.7 cm) from the edge, and make a single backstitch to end seam.

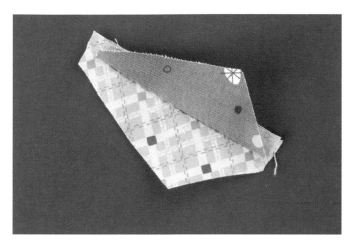

5. Press the piece open. Repeat process until four sets are completed.

6. Sew the four sets together into the inner star. Press all seam allowances in the same direction.

7. Sew B and C (and B1 and C1) pieces together. Then, sew together along C and C1 seam line to make a corner block.

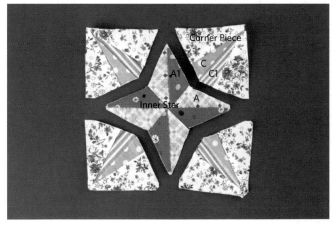

8. Make four corner pieces. Lay out the inner star and corner pieces into the star design.

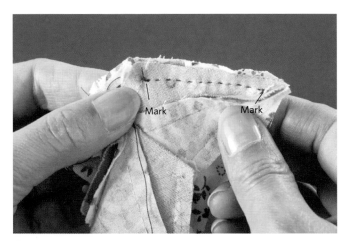

9. With right sides together, align a corner piece with one side of the inner star. Starting from the outside edge, sew to the mark where pieces A, A1, C, and C1 meet.

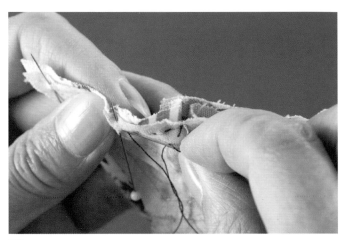

10. Keep the seam allowance free and continue sewing the rest of the seam to the other outside edge. Repeat process until all four corner pieces are attached to the inner star.

11. Completed star block. Press using the iron.

Quilting Basics

How to draw quilting lines and baste.

1. Using a pencil with a soft lead (such as 2B), draw the quilting lines on the right side of the quilt top.

Quilt top (right side)

Batting

Backing (wrong side)

2. Cut the batting and backing ¾" to 1¼" (2-3 cm) [2¼" to 2¾" (6-7 cm) for bigger pieces] larger than the quilt top. Layer the quilt top, batting, and backing, and secure with pins. Baste to secure the three layers.

Basting order

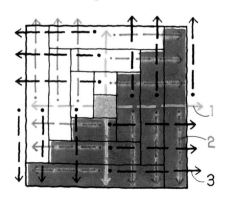

Always baste from the center towards the outside of the quilt. This will prevent the layers from shifting as you work.

How to quilt.

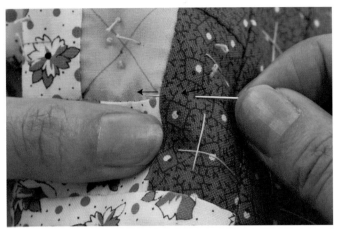

1. Start quilting from the center of the block. Thread a quilting needle and make a knot at the end of the thread. Insert the needle into the quilt top and draw out where you want to start.

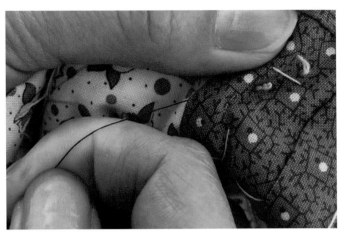

2. Tug the thread to pull the knot into the batting.

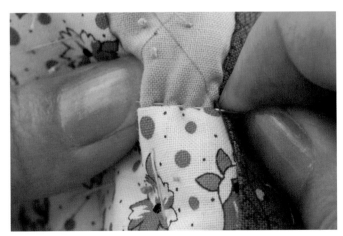

3. Make running stitches, catching the batting and the backing. This is called quilting.

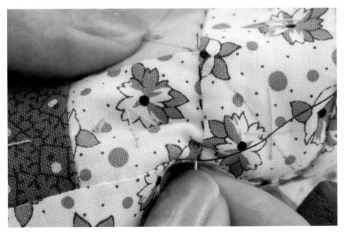

4. When the center piece is quilted, insert the needle into the fabric, traveling under the top fabric layer only, draw out the needle, and start quilting the next piece.

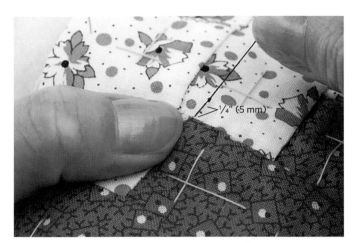

5. At the end of the thread, make a knot ¼" (5 mm) from the last stitch.

6. Insert the needle at the same spot where you finished the running stitch. Traveling underneath the top fabric layer only, draw out the needle ⅜" (1 cm) away. Tug the thread to pull the knot into the batting. With the thread held taut, cut it short so that the end stays inside the batting.

7. When the quilting is completed, remove the basting stitches.

Quilting order

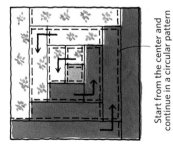

Stitch in the ditch

Start from the center and continue in a circular pattern

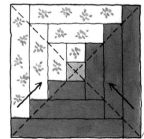

Other quilting
(Lattice and outline quilt)

Start quilting from the edge

How to mark and trim the excess seam allowance.

1. Draw a square border on the right side of the quilt top. Draw straight lines using a ruler. For a curved design such as the bottom of a bag, mark using the pattern template.

2. Baste the layers together around the entire quilt, using a ³⁄₈" (1 cm) seam allowance. This basting is a guideline for attaching the binding.

3. Trim the excess batting and backing.

Basting around the entire quilt, as in step 2, will prevent the quilt edges from stretching as the binding is attached.

How to make a bias strip and sew the binding.

Short bindings

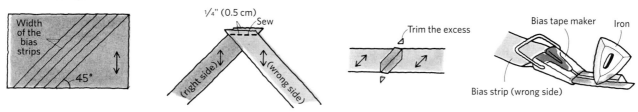

Fold the fabric on the bias and make a fold line at 45°. Draw lines parallel to the fold line and cut. You may need to attach a few bias strips, as shown above, to make the binding the correct length. Pass the fabric though a bias tape maker and press to make the fold line.

Long bindings

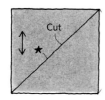
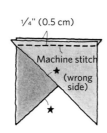
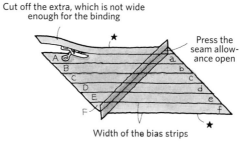
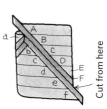

Starting with a square piece of fabric, cut on the diagonal line, then sew the crosswise edges with right sides together. Draw lines the desired width of the bias tape. With right sides together, fold fabric into a tube with one strip width extending beyond the edge on each side. Stitch. Starting at one end, cut bias tape in one continuous strip.

How to attach a bias binding to a quilt.

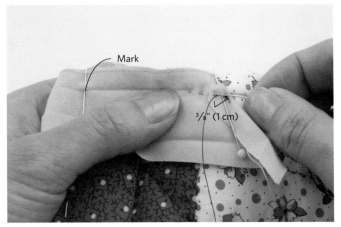

1. Unfold the bias strip and with right sides together, align the bias strip with the raw edge of the quilt top. Fold ³⁄₈" (1 cm) of the short edge of the bias strip and start sewing. Make sure to position the start of the bias binding away from the corner in order to reduce seam allowance bulk.

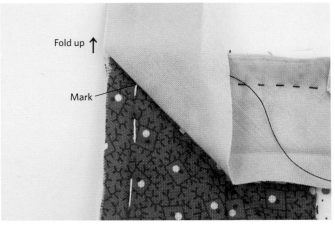

2. Fold the binding up and away from the quilt, creating a 45° angle. Crease.

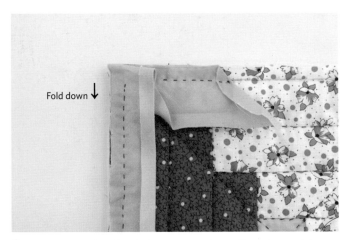

3. Fold the binding back down over the 45° angle, making a horizontal fold even with the quilt top. Sew from mark to mark. Finish sewing bias strips to all four sides, repeating process at corners.

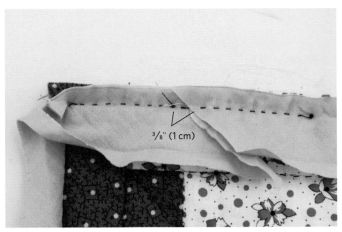

4. Overlap ³⁄₈" (1 cm) of the edges of the bias strip.

5. Turn the binding right side out, including the frame corners, without unfolding them.

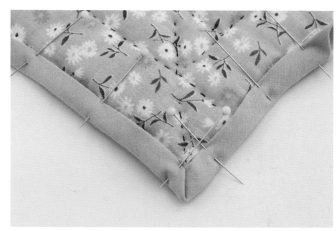

6. Fold the corner and secure with pins.

7. Make a small hemstitch, attaching the binding to the backing.

8. Finished binding

Index

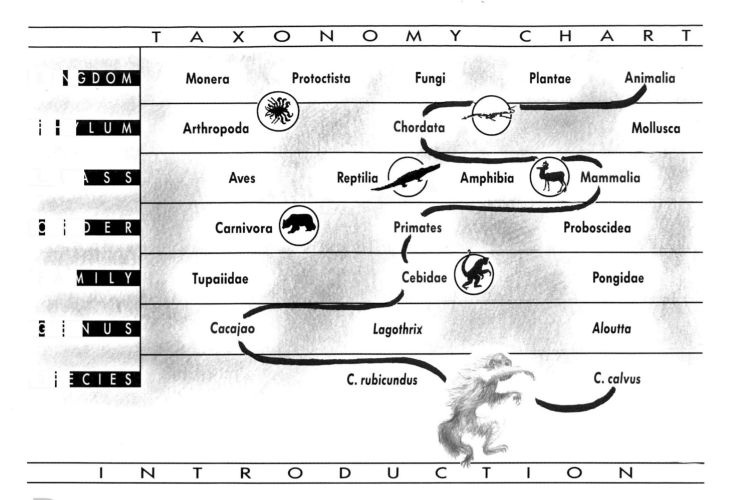

KINGDOM	Monera	Protoctista	Fungi	Plantae	Animalia
PHYLUM	Arthropoda		Chordata		Mollusca
CLASS	Aves	Reptilia	Amphibia		Mammalia
ORDER	Carnivora		Primates		Proboscidea
FAMILY	Tupaiidae		Cebidae		Pongidae
GENUS	Cacajao		Lagothrix		Aloutta
SPECIES		C. rubicundus			C. calvus

I N T R O D U C T I O N

P rimates (we humans are primates!) belong to the scientific class Mammalia and share common characteristics with other mammals. All mammals have hair or fur, nurse their young, and have a constant internal body temperature, which means they are homoiothermic. (Reptiles and amphibians, in contrast, depend on their outside environment for body heat.)

Lemurs, black-handed spider monkeys, orangutans, and humans are all primates. Although we may look different from one another, we have much in common. All primates have flexible hands (usually with ten digits) and opposable thumbs and fingers that can grasp objects. We have relatively large, complex brains. And at one time, all primates were tree-dwellers.

Primates vary in size from a few ounces to half a ton! Although human primates live everywhere in the world, most nonhuman primates live in tropical or subtropical regions. Many primate species are endangered by modern dilemmas such as pollution and loss of living space. All nonhuman primates need to be treated with respect by human primates. There are about 180 species of primates.

Scientists use a universal system to keep track of primates and the millions of plant and animal species on earth. The system is a science called taxonomy. It is a way of grouping or classifying things. Taxonomy starts with the five main groups of all living things, the kingdoms, and then divides those into the next group down, phylum, then class, order, family, genus, and, finally, species. Members of a species look similar, and they can reproduce with each other.

For an example of how taxonomy works, look at the highlighted lines above to see how the white uakari is classified.

As you learn about the primates in this book, look for the scientific name in parentheses after the common name. The first word is the genus; the second word is the species.

Turn to the *glossarized index* at the back of this book if you're looking for a specific primate, for special information (what does prehensile mean, for instance), or for the definition of a word you don't understand.

Mini Mouse

Gray Lesser Mouse Lemur *(Microcebus murinus)*

Primates! If some monkeys threw a primate party, the invitation list would include bush babies, sakis, monkeys, apes, chimpanzees, and you and me.

What do we all have in common? Flexible hands with grasping fingers (usually with ten digits), relatively large brains, and a tree-dwelling life-style at some point in our evolution.

Of course, you would have some extremely weird dancing partners. Certain primates sport blue cheeks or red rear ends, while others wear punk hairdos. And they range in size from several ounces to more than 500 pounds. Watch out for your toes!

MARY SUNDSTROM

Mouse lemurs are pocket-sized critters, one of the world's smallest primates. They're also one of the oldest: their ancestors were among the very first primates on earth.

Mouse lemurs have a sweet tooth for fruit and honey, and insects are a favorite food. When eating beetles and grasshoppers, lemurs bite the soft belly of the bug first and make noisy smacking sounds. Lemurs are active during the day or night, depending on their species. To communicate with each other, lemurs chirrup, chatter, and even yodel from the tree of their choice.

Not all lemurs are tiny. In fact, they vary from rat to cat size. There are about 20 different types of lemurs, and they all live on Madagascar, a big island off the coast of Africa.

Ancient Romans believed the spirits of their dead roamed the night staring at the living with round glowing eyes and crying sadly. They called those ghosts "lemurs."

Sifakas are closely related to lemurs. Island natives believed these animals were sacred sun worshipers because they rise early to sunbathe in the trees.

The Prosimians may sound like a group of musicians or a football team, but they actually make up the largest group of primates. Prosimians look a lot like their primitive ancestors. Members of this group include lemurs, lorises, and tarsiers.

SALLY BLAKEMORE

PRIMATES

Slow Loris *(Nycticebus coucang)*

This slowpoke prosimian would never be seen without its thick fur coat. Even at home in the tropics of Africa and Asia, the loris would die of cold without all of its fur. That's because a loris produces very little body heat energy. Low energy means a lazy routine and no fast footwork for these compact mammals. The slow loris dangles easily from branches and moves at a sloth's pace.

Lorises have bright big eyes that can see after dark, which is when they search for a variety of insects, birds, and eggs to eat. They have such short tails hidden under their fur, they are almost tailless. Thumbs and big toes point away from fingers and smaller toes, which means they are super opposable and able to grasp branches and twigs —just like your hands.

If you asked primates for a show of hands, they would all hold up their movable fingers. Some primates, chimpanzees, and humans, for example, can pick up a toothpick or a twig between their fingers and thumb. A loris uses its hand like a clamp to get a grip. Tree shrews have claws, and they use them to dig into branches. It might seem like a simple thing, but the ability to wrap fingers (and toes) around a branch is what made primates the masters of the trees. Because our ancestors developed this ability, they could climb higher without falling, reach more food, and grow bigger!

When a slow loris twitters like a scolding bird, that's the signal that it is annoyed! To avoid danger, a slow loris will back its way up a tree, step by step.

Primates can be divided into four groups—prosimians, New World monkeys, Old World monkeys, and the great apes. Humans belong to the same group as apes. Primatologists (scientists who study primates) believe both humans and apes shared a common ancestor about 20 million years ago.

What was the original primate ancestor like? By studying existing prosimians and ancient fossils, primatologists are getting a pretty clear picture.

PRIMATES

Photo, facing page, © Zoological Society of San Diego, photo by Ron Garrison

Philippine Tarsier (*Tarsius syrichta*)

What is forty million years old, has huge saucer eyes, a hairy nose, and pop eyes in the back of its head? What else? A tiny tarsier.

Actually, a tarsier's eyes are located on either side of its nose, just like human eyes.

But tarsiers can swivel their necks 180 degrees so they can see who's sneaking up from behind. Gotcha!

These mighty mini-animals are among the smallest of all monkey species. They weigh about 4½ ounces, about the size of a guinea pig. Babies are mouse-sized, and they cling to their mothers from birth, chirping noisily. When they're in a hurry, mothers also carry their babies by mouth, just like cats do, or they plop them on a handy branch when they go hunting.

Tarsiers are mighty leapers and can jump from tree to tree in the tropical forests of Southeast Asia where they live. Grown-up tarsiers can leap long distances and land on their two hind feet. In midair, they keep arms and legs close to their bodies and use their tails to steer. When they come down to earth, tarsiers leap like frogs.

When they're not jumping, they're often grooming fellow tarsiers. For primates, grooming means more than removing ticks, mites, and dirt. It's a way of learning who's who in the social order of a primate group.

When native headhunters of Borneo went on the warpath, it was bad luck to spot a tarsier. Hunters believed it meant they would lose their own heads because tarsiers can swivel theirs.

When tarsiers are excited, their big ears don't stop moving. In fact, they move in two directions at once: while one ear turns forward, the other turns back.

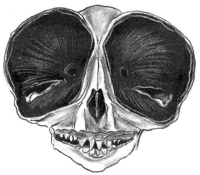

Tarsier eyes are largest in proportion to their body size of all primates. If human eyes were proportionately as pop-eyed, we would be looking at the world through grapefruits!

Jumbo eyes! Each eye is about the same size as the tarsier's brain. They use their big eyes to hunt insects and lizards at night. These are the only primates who restrict their diet to live prey.

PRIMATES

Photo, facing page, © Zoological Society of San Diego, photo by Ron Garrison

Pygmy Marmoset (*Callithrix pygmaea*)

Tucked among tree branches in the forests of the upper Amazon, the olive-colored pygmy marmoset sounds a lot like a bird when it chirrups, twitters, and chik-chiks. There are six to eight types of marmosets—in a variety of colors and sizes. Some have naked faces in gold or black, some have great moustaches, and others sport fuzzy beards. Marmosets are agile monkeys, and they have claws instead of nails on the ends of their fingers. These claws give them a no-slip grip on branches.

Some marmosets grow as large as hefty rats and fat cats, but the pygmy marmoset, only 3 ounces when fully grown, is as small as the mouse lemur. Like all marmosets, pygmies are diurnal, which means they rise and shine with the sun. They spend lots of their day socializing with other pygmy marmosets. They are brave little critters, but they don't look for a fight. If something makes them nervous, they might scurry up the nearest tree like a squirrel. And if they're really scared, their hair stands straight up on their heads.

When a prosimian wants to reach out and catch something, it doesn't have an easy task. Prosimians can move their fingers and toes easily, but all five digits move together. If one finger grabs, they all grab. This is called "whole-hand control." Think about that the next time you try to thread a needle or play a guitar.

Through evolution, primates became better equipped for life in trees. They needed sharp eyes for spying fruit and more brain space to remember where and when it would be ripe. Instead of eyes on the sides of their heads (like horses), primate eyes slowly moved forward for 3-D vision. Areas of the brain devoted to vision and memory got bigger, while smelling centers did not. Just try smelling your way around your house!

PRIMATES

Golden-lion Tamarin *(Leontopithecus rosalia)*

When golden-lion tamarins feel threatened, it's no secret. Their silky golden hair stands up, they make wild faces, and they shriek. (They may sound like some human primates you know.)

These tamarins are monkeys. Their gray hairless faces are oddly human, and their eyes are a piercing blue.

Generally, tamarins get along with the other types of monkeys that share their tree homes in Brazilian rain forests. They chatter and chirp and spring through the higher branches of tall trees in search of fruits and insects to eat. These animals are curious and lively and very excitable.

Like many primates, golden-lion tamarins are endangered. As humans cut down the rain forests to build houses, farm, and graze livestock, this primate's habitat disappears, and fewer and fewer survive in the wild. Fortunately, there are now protected reserves for these animals. Some zoos also have special programs to breed tamarins in captivity and return them to the wild (as long as there's a wild to return them to).

Golden-lion tamarins have long, elegant fingers that are partly webbed.

When baby tamarins are nursing, they cling to their mothers. But the rest of the time, fathers take over child care. They even mash up fruit for babies to eat.

12

PRIMATES

White-faced Saki (*Pithecia pithecia*)

The dot-eyed white-faced saki wears a woebegone expression under its shaggy hood of hair. This shy and sensitive New World monkey makes its home in the highest trees of South American forests. There, it can stride along thin branches like a tightrope walker, standing tall, hands held out for balance, and fingers spread. A saki is quickest when it moves on all fours and leaps from branch to branch.

If sakis stand on two feet and shake their fur, watch out. That's a good sign these monkeys are upset.

When it's time to sleep at night, white-faced sakis curl up like cats among the branches. To reach fruit, berries, and leaves, some types of sakis hang by their hind feet and munch contentedly.

Sakis come with a few variations: there are very hairy ones, and some with beards and red noses. These are animals who need plenty of space, privacy, and trees.

Sakis don't mind getting their feet wet, but their beard is another matter. To drink from streams, sakis often dip their hands into water and then lick their wet fur.

New World monkeys live in South and Central America. Some have prehensile tails that can reach and grab like a third arm. None have tough "sitting pads" on their rear ends like Old World monkeys.

PRIMATES

Photo, facing page, courtesy Animals Animals © Bates Littlehales

Weird Wah-CAR-ee!

White Uakari (*Cacajao calvus*)

With naked pink faces and ears, stumpy tails, and wispy hair, uakaris are the weirdest of the weird-looking. Large troops of uakaris roam the branches of the Brazilian rain forest where they spend almost all their time. When the rainy season floods the jungle floor, they don't even touch ground to gather fallen fruits. These cat-sized animals are the only short-tailed monkeys in the Americas. Although their six-inch tails aren't very impressive, uakaris do have long, furry fingers and toes.

Uakaris are often quiet, but they can communicate with loud, hysterical-sounding shrieks, almost as if they're laughing. They are playful, like many monkeys, and the young make up games to amuse themselves.

At one time, native hunters in South American rain forests used blow darts, poisoned with the mucous of frogs, to catch uakaris. When the dart struck its target, the monkeys were paralyzed and fell from the trees. Hunters would sometimes use salt to counteract the poison. Baby uakaris were often kept as pets, but adults were eaten.

In the Middle Ages, physicians dissected the bodies of monkeys so they could learn more about human anatomy. In those days, dissecting a human body for medical purposes was strictly against the rules.

Captive primates can be more aggressive than their relatives in the wild. That's because they are forced to live in small spaces and compete for food. Human primates in big cities are usually more aggressive and grumpy than their country cousins.

PRIMATES

Monkey Business

Black-handed Spider Monkey *(Ateles geoffroyi)*

Spider monkeys, who are found in southern Mexico, through Colombia, Venezuela, and the Amazon Basin, are swinging superstars able to travel in jungle treetops using sure-grip fingers and toes, long arms and legs, and a grabby tail. Spider monkey tails are prehensile, a fancy word for grasping that rhymes with "utensil." Tails come in handy to keep monkeys from falling out of trees when they're asleep. They also keep food and other monkeys within a tail's length, which is longer than an arm's length.

Black-faced, with flesh-colored goggles and white-rimmed eyes, spider monkeys travel in troops of up to 25 individuals. During the day, they search for fresh fruit and nuts. These monkeys are very picky about the fruit they eat. They pinch, sniff, and taste the goods just like some very particular human shoppers.

Spider monkeys must always be on the alert for hungry predators like eagles and jaguars. When threatened, they will scratch their fur nervously and bark like a dog. They will also break off branches (some weighing as much as 10 pounds) and drop them on whoever lurks below.

What's in a name? Spider monkeys are so named because of their long spidery limbs and tail. Also, their knobby joints stick up when they're scurrying along branches so they resemble arachnids with five legs instead of eight!

A spider monkey's tail is so sensitive, it can pick up a peanut.

When rain forest natives went hunting with poison darts, many spider monkeys didn't fall out of trees after they were shot. That's because they were so firmly attached to branches by hands, feet, and tail.

PRIMATES

DeBrazza's Guenon *(Cercopithecus neglectus)*

Thumbs up! DeBrazza's babies suck their thumbs just like human babies.

Spiked, buzzed, and streaked, guenons are some of the flashiest and punkiest monkeys in Africa! They use their colorful faces, as well as head movements, to spot their own kind and to communicate. An up-and-down jerk of the head may mean keep away, while a yawn says, "I'm the boss." Guenons send messages in living color, too. One type of guenon sports a blue mask around its eyes. When it gets excited, the mask turns even bluer—because there's more blood circulating. Of course, humans change colors, too. Some people turn very pink when they're embarrassed.

Guenon monkeys come in a rainbow of colorful designs. Some have blue bottoms, red stripes, red ears, and speckled fur. Others are green with red tails. Or wear yellow whiskers or a white oval nose spot. Some have beards, and others have great tufts of hair on their heads.

With puffy cheeks, white chin whiskers, a white upper lip and throat, an orange-patched forehead, a black mane, and black arms and legs, the DeBrazza's are the most colorful of all guenon monkeys. They gallop on all fours, with their tails held proudly in the air like flags. These fruit, nut, and insect gourmets live in the rain forests of the African Congo.

Guenons spend much of their time in a forest of trees, leaping limb to limb. But they do come down to earth to search for jumpy critters like crickets and grasshoppers, their favorite snack.

Old World monkeys, like the guenons, live in Africa, Southeast Asia, and the Malay Archipelago. They have tough pads (like calluses) on their rumps so they can sleep sitting up in trees.

PRIMATES

Patas Monkey (*Erythrocebus patas*)

Troops of muscular, long-legged, red-haired patas monkeys roam the grasslands and deserts of equatorial Africa searching for food—leaves, roots, fruit, insects, beans, seeds, lizards, young birds, and eggs.

Female patas monkeys grow to be 1½ feet tall. These little she-monkeys act as leaders of the troop when the males are busy watching for predators. Adult males are twice as big as females, and one of them always has the job of troop "watch monkey." Other bachelor males travel in their own groups separate from the main troop.

Patas monkeys are not aggressive fighters, and they don't organize against their enemies. When they're threatened, they often crouch down in tall grasses to hide. Sometimes the males will run away to lead predators away from females and baby monkeys.

Nonhuman primates all over the world are threatened by loss of habitat. When humans move into forests, grasslands, and onto mountains, wild creatures must move out. Since we share a very small planet, our primate relatives are running out of living space. Eventually, we humans will face the same problem unless we slow down our population growth.

Three amazing female primates have spent much of their lives learning about great apes. Jane Goodall studies chimpanzees in Tanzania. Birute Galdikas observes orangutans in Borneo. The late Dian Fossey fought to save the mountain gorillas of Rwanda. They all share a deep love for, and commitment to, the great apes.

PRIMATES

Sulawesi Crested Macaque (*Macaca nigra*)

On the Indonesian island of Sulawesi, 10-pound to 25-pound monkeys the color of ebony, with crested hair and pink padded rumps, raise their families peacefully.

At first glance, it's easy to mistake a crested macaque for a baboon. They both walk on all fours, and their pointy skulls are shaped with the same thick protruding eyebrows. But crested macaques are quieter and more easygoing than their baboon relatives.

No one is really sure how the crested macaque first came to the island of Sulawesi. Some say they traveled from the Philippines long, long ago. Now, the crested macaque has only one home, Sulawesi.

To see how important opposable thumbs are, try climbing a tree or picking fruit without using your thumbs!

Some native tribes on Sulawesi worship the crested macaque because they believe these primates are their ancestors. When they fill river rafts with food and set them adrift, they are paying homage to the gods of the apes.

Sulawesi crested macaques look a little like cone heads. As these primates grow older, their hair stands straighter and pointier. If they get excited, it really stands up!

24

PRIMATES

Gelada (*Theropithecus gelada*)

Rough, tough, and hefty, geladas are fierce troopers. The ruff of hair around an adult male's shoulders makes him look even tougher and heftier than his 45 to 60 pounds of muscle. Since these monkeys have come down from the trees to spend most of their lives on the ground, they have developed new ways to defend themselves from predators like lions, hyenas, and especially leopards.

Long teeth, strong jaws, and powerful shoulder muscles provide protection, and organized group defense gives them power in numbers against any common enemy except humans.

Geladas have thick lustrous coats and naked bright red chests. They live at high elevations where food is scarce. Most of their diet consists of grass, roots and all. But they also eat seeds, leaves, onions, and occasional insects—almost anything they can find. Geladas are formidable fighters. To ward off enemies, they will throw stones or roll rocks downhill. Geladas are not fond of their relatives, hamadryas baboons.

Primates are amazingly strong. A 45-pound gelada male has the strength of a human male who is three to six times bigger!

Baboons are close relatives of geladas. Baboons love babies—anybody's! Adults in the troop act as grandparents, aunts, and uncles, sharing food, grooming fur, and cuddling babies in their laps.

Baboon babies have it made in the shade! While grown-up baboons go off to hunt for food, baboon babies spend their time up a tree swinging, climbing, and monkeying around. A few older baboon "baby-sitters" stay behind to look after things. The tree not only makes a great jungle gym to play on but it also keeps babies off the ground and safe from hungry predators.

PRIMATES

Japanese Macaque or Snow Monkey (*Macaca fuscata*)

Shy snow monkeys go to great depths to stay warm. They spend winter hours soaking in thermal hot springs located in the mountain forests of Japan where they live. In these steamy natural pools, they continue daily life, nursing their babies, grooming, and schooling.

Shaggy, long fur coats help keep snow monkeys warm when they're not in hot water, and cheek pouches are handy for storing food. These macaques sleep in trees at night and wander in search of shoots, buds, and roots during the day. They travel in troops of 30 to 150 members. When they stop to feed, they form two circles. Young male snow monkeys stay on the outer circle. They are the first line of defense against predators. Females, babies, and adult males of high social rank form the inner circle. A dominant male is the most powerful member of the troop. When young monkeys wrestle, play tag, and roughhouse with each other, they also learn their place in the social order.

Japanese scientists spent many years studying snow monkeys. They found these primates use as many as 30 different sounds to communicate with each other. They also watched as snow monkeys learned to do new things. Swimming, for instance. Scientists used peanuts to encourage a few monkeys to go into the ocean. Soon, the snow monkeys had learned to swim and even dive!

One day, a young female snow monkey dipped a sandy sweet potato in water and decided it tasted better clean. A month later, one of her friends washed a sweet potato. Four years later, 15 monkeys were washing potatoes. Nine years later, half of the snow monkeys were doing the same! That's probably how humans learned to wash potatoes thousands of years ago—from the younger generation.

Snow monkeys are part of Japanese art, folklore, and myth. They are the three monkeys who "see no evil, hear no evil, and speak no evil," representing the wisdom of Buddha.

PRIMATES

28

350 17 869

Mandrill *(Mandrillus sphinx)*

A red nose, bright blue cheeks, a yellow beard and shoulder ruff, and a purply-red rear end are a male mandrill's everyday colors. These dog-faced forest monkeys from western Central Africa reach heights of 2½ feet and weigh in at 55 pounds, and their large bodies are packed with muscle. When provoked, mandrills are as strong as gorillas or leopards.

You can't miss an angry mandrill. His rainbow face turns even brighter colors when more blood circulates, and he yawns to show off four-inch yellow fangs.

When most monkeys show their teeth, watch out! A grin or grimace equals fear in mandrill language. It's easy to believe those fangs are less than friendly.

Ants, beetles, and other insects are mandrill delicacies, and fruits and vegetables are staples. But when they're really hungry, almost anything will do.

Female mandrills and their babies hang out in trees, while male mandrills spend most of their day on the ground. In battle—fighting predators or rival males—mandrills are ferocious, but they can also be gentle and affectionate with each other.

Troops of mandrills, like baboons, maintain a definite hierarchy, or power structure. Chief males spend most of their time with chief females. Their offspring usually inherit their favored positions in mandrill society. Less powerful mandrills act in more submissive roles.

Mandrills walk on all twenty—fingers and toes, that is. They never let the palms of their hands or feet touch the ground.

PRIMATES

Proboscis Monkey (*Nasalis larvatus*)

Honk kee-honk, Cyrano of the swampy Borneo rain forest has arrived! Male proboscis monkeys sport a schnozz that just won't stop—growing, that is. If a proboscis monkey is lucky, his nose will grow to lengths of four inches—so long, it overhangs his mouth. To female monkeys, the longer the male's nose, the stronger the sex appeal.

Proboscis monkeys grow to be as tall as 2½ feet from head to toe, and they may weigh as much as 50 pounds. They honk (males kee-honk) when they're happily eating leaves, shoots, and assorted fruits or catching sun rays. To relax or nap, they stretch out on their backs. Baby proboscis monkeys like to spend their play time swinging from grown-up tails or squeezing the biggest nose that's handy.

Proboscis monkeys live in very flexible social groups. The button-eyed male proboscis monkeys are famous for their grand noses and pinkish brown faces, but all babies begin life with small noses and deep blue faces.

Proboscis monkeys get their name from a Latin word for an elephant's trunk. Their noses are fleshy and flexible, and some are so long, they get in the way when these animals eat or drink.

Proboscis monkeys love to get into the swim. They high-dive 50 feet from trees, swim under water, and dogpaddle across streams, lakes, and even oceans. Waterlogged proboscis monkeys have been rescued far from ocean shores by fishing boats.

The nose of the male proboscis monkey keeps growing its entire life. Because females prefer to mate with the longest-nosed males, evolution ensures that proboscis monkeys will remain Cyrano of the rain forest.

PRIMATES

Drill *(Mandrillus leucophaeus)*

Drills, like their close relatives the mandrills, will eat almost anything. A drill smorgasbord includes roots, fruit, plants, snails, lizards, insects, mice, snakes, frogs, and worms for dessert!

When troops of five to fifty drills are wandering among the trees of a forest, they like to stay in constant contact with each other. To do this, they keep up steady grunting and snorting noises. Even if they can't be seen, they're heard! Drills also chatter and make faces when they're flustered. If they're really upset, they may run around shrieking.

When a 60-pound drill gives a friendly shake of the head and shoulders, that's a request to be groomed. Hopefully, another drill will carefully remove bugs, ticks, and mites from its fur. When grooming others, a drill will press its teeth together and make loud smacking noises of satisfaction. A small smile with chattering teeth is a friendly greeting that says, "I feel good."

Angry drills and mandrills are easy to spot. They slap the ground with one hand while the hair on their neck stands up. The colored areas on their bodies turn even brighter. They never take their eyes from whoever is upsetting them. They also spread their arms, lower their heads, and flash their powerful teeth in a big yawn. This is called "threat posture." It's a way of telling someone, "Watch out, I'm warning you!" After giving this behavior several tries, these animals may sit down and scratch their arms and thighs energetically. Or, they may attack!

Drills and mandrills are known to live as long as forty years, maybe more!

Ancient Egyptians trained hamadryas baboons to do their simple chores like collecting firewood and harvesting cultivated figs. They also worshiped the "smartest" of these baboons, giving them special tasks to perform in temples. Some were even mummified and buried with pharaohs.

Have you ever seen a snail playing? Probably not. Playing around is something only mammals seem to do. We humans play a lot, especially when we're young. And so do primates! Just watch a baby chimpanzee, baboon, or gorilla.

PRIMATES

The Duke

Douc Langur *(Pygathrix nemaeus)*

As regal as Asian royalty, the douc langur lives quietly and peacefully in the rain forests of Vietnam and Laos. This unusual and beautiful primate looks at the world through dark, almond eyes. Its soft, glossy fur, colorful markings, and white beard add to its mysterious appeal.

The Vietnamese word for monkey is *douc* (pronounced "duke"). Sadly, these monkeys are in danger of becoming extinct. The Vietnam War can be blamed for many of their woes. Bombs and chemical weapons destroyed much of their homeland, and soldiers living in the jungles hunted them for meat. War causes so much suffering for humans, sometimes we forget that thousands of other living creatures are also harmed.

To learn about primates, find a group that you can observe for six hours. Sit quietly watching. (Of course, you'll have to take breaks now and then!) You'll see how smart they are, who's in command, who's friendly and who's not. In the wild, primates can avoid conflict because they have room to move. In zoos, they must learn to live together. How would you survive if you had to live in a cage with a bunch of strangers?

The white-headed langur was discovered in 1952 in a rain forest in China. Now, only a few hundred of these monkeys remain, and they live on just 200 square miles of forest. They are hunted locally and eaten as a health tonic. There are many wildlife conservation groups working to save endangered primates all over the world. Joining a conservation group is one way you can help.

36

PRIMATES

Photo, facing page, © Zoological Society of San Diego, photo by Ron Garrison

Orangutan *(Pongo pygmaeus)*

Gorillas, chimpanzees, and orangutans are "great apes." Because of their anatomy and their mental capacities, they are the most humanlike of all animals. In fact, they are our closest relatives. Among this group, the orangutan is the only true tree-dwelling ape.

The orangutan, which sports a shaggy reddish mop, naked ears, mobile lips, and woeful eyes, lives quietly in the trees of the rain forests of Borneo and Sumatra. Although orangs are big—adult males may weigh 200 pounds and females about 90—they are hard to spot in the high branches. Scientists used to think these "shy" orangutans were antisocial, but now they know better.

Orangutans have social relationships very much like other apes, only their interaction moves in slow motion. Although adult male orangutans do lead very solitary lives, adult females keep each other company, adolescents (like human teenagers) love to hang out with their peers, and mothers are devoted to their babies.

An orang mother will nurse, cuddle, and clean her baby. She washes it with rain water and trims its fingernails with her teeth. Just like a human infant, a baby orangutan is helpless and cries when it is cold or hungry or tired.

A baby orangutan gestates in its mother's womb for almost eight months. Young orangs sometimes nurse as long as three years. While nursing their young, adult females cannot get pregnant. That means a female orangutan might have five babies in her 40-year lifetime, but because many baby orangs die in the wild, only two or three will survive.

Although orangutans are now protected by law, they are still in danger of becoming extinct because much of their habitat is disappearing through human activities like logging and farming.

When standing, an orangutan's arms can reach its ankles. Some orang's arms have an eight-foot spread!

In the Malayan language, the word *orang-utan* means "forest man." Orangutans are creatures of the jungle, where their only enemy is man.

When captive orangutans are rescued, they must take a course on jungle survival before they are returned to the wild. Many captive orangs were just babies when their parents were killed and they were kidnapped. There are a few special programs where young orangutans relearn their roots.

Orangutans don't know how to swim, but they're not afraid of water, and they will wade across deep streams and rivers.

Photo, facing page, © Zoological Society of San Diego. photo by Ken Kelley

PRIMATES

Pygmy Chimpanzee *(Pan paniscus)*

Pygmy chimps live only in the tropical rain forests of Zaire, Africa. These animals weigh in at 80 to 100 pounds, while regular chimpanzees are about 10 pounds heavier. All chimpanzees, from the lowland forests to the grasslands of equatorial Africa, are endangered because of human activities. Chimps are hunted for food and sport and trapped for medical research. The United States, Japan, and Europe are the main purchasers of captive chimps even though most trade is illegal!

When genes of chimps and humans are compared, it's clear that we are blood cousins. Of all the great apes, chimps are closest to humans in behavior. Chimps use tools. In the wild, they gather small sticks to search for termites and use crumpled leaves for sponges. In captivity, they've learned to open locks with keys, pound nails with hammers, wash and brush their hair, and answer a ringing phone and say, "Boo."

When scientists test their intelligence, chimps rate well. These animals are outgoing, curious, and willing to please. Chimpanzees have even learned to say words like "mama" and "cup"—and to use them correctly. Generally, scientists say chimps are smart but not as smart as humans. But what do scientific tests of great apes really prove?

If you were caught by a group of apes and sent to Africa to live in a tree, how "smart" would you be? How would you know which plants to eat without getting sick? Could you follow a scent trail with your nose? Would you be able to communicate with your captors? After all, it's not easy to measure intelligence.

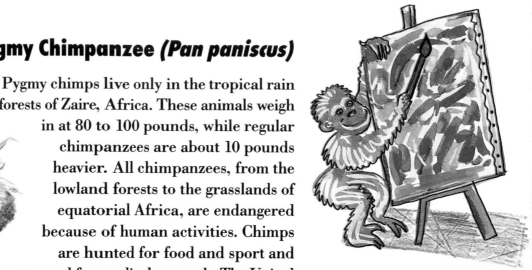

When captive chimps are given a pencil and paper and begin to draw, move over, Picasso! In 1971, a chimp named June had a one-chimp show at an art gallery in Chicago. Years earlier, two chimps, Congo and Betsy, had their work displayed at the Institute of Contemporary Art in London.

Chimps are capable of a wide array of emotions. They hug, kiss, and hold hands with their chimp friends. And they express other emotions just like humans do. When they're thoughtful, angry, happy, or afraid, chimps and humans make similar faces. When sad, a chimp looks like a crying child—except chimps can't shed tears.

PRIMATES

Lowland Gorilla *(Gorilla gorilla gorilla)*

These gentle giants from Africa can reach a height of more than 5 feet, and one 300-pound gorilla may be as strong as 10 humans. But gorillas are not the "monsters" that run rampant on the late-late show. In fact, unless gorillas think their families are in danger, they are very peaceable.

Gorillas live in small groups, and they often mingle peacefully with other gorilla families. When a male gorilla is between 11 and 13 years old, he grows silver hairs on his back. This silver-back can then become the leader of his own family group. When he wants to scare off intruders or remind his family who's the boss, the silver-back begins by screaming, then bites a leaf between his lips. Standing on his hind legs, tossing twigs into the air, he beats his great chest. For a finale, he tears out grass and plants, runs around on all fours, and beats the floor with his hand. (If that seems strange, just watch a human primate on the dance floor.)

Gorillas have been tested for intelligence by human standards. Some are as "smart" as human kids. Gorillas certainly do lots of "people" things—or maybe people do lots of "gorilla" things. They clean their ears and pick their noses with their index fingers. They yawn, burp, hiccough, scratch, and huff and puff. Mothers kiss babies, and babies climb onto their father's lap. They use at least 22 sounds to communicate with each other.

Gorillas are rare and endangered because humans are moving into their homeland. Also, poachers often kill entire gorilla families in order to capture one baby. Although gorillas (and other great apes) are not human, many people believe that killing them is murder. These people are working hard to make sure great apes will not become extinct.

Gorillas are known to catch small animals like lizards and frogs in the wild and "pet" them gently.

Gorillas are complete vegetarians. They not only eat plants, they also wear big leaves on their heads as decoration.

One of a gorilla's favorite treats is wild celery.

Besides 10,000 lowland gorillas, there are less than 350 mountain gorillas left on earth. These primates live in a small area of Africa called the Virunga Volcano region. Many conservation groups are working hard to protect these gorillas from poachers and to provide money for primate research. But we must hurry!

PRIMATES

Photo, facing page, © Zoological Society of San Diego, photo by Ron Garrison

Humans (*Homo sapiens*)

Humans are primates. In fact, we belong to the same primate group as apes do, and most scientists believe we shared a common ancestor who roamed the earth about 20 million years ago. But humans are special—at least we think we are. Why?

Because we're smart? True, humans have great brain power, but our big brains are only a few hundred thousand years old, and apes aren't far behind us. Even though they don't have a formal language, apes can learn from experience and make logical decisions, they understand abstract ideas, and they make and use simple tools that help free them from the limits of their environment.

Because we're curious? As humans, we always try to find new and "better" technology. This quality has been crucial to our own evolution as a species. But many animals are curious. Chimpanzees, especially. And some scientists believe that human "curiosity" is very primitive because we make things just because we can— without thinking if we really should.

Because we appreciate art? Humans do create wonderful works of art. We write symphonies, we sing the blues, we paint murals, and we build cathedrals. But drawings by primates are much like drawings by human children. And just as some kids grow up to become famous artists, the art of non-human primates will also evolve over time. There are already famous chimpanzee artists.

Because we love beauty? Chimpanzees have been known to spend 15 minutes observing a beautiful sunset!

Let's face it, *nonhuman* primates are special! Sadly, as they become extinct, humans are learning about habitat balance. If we cannot make room for these wonderful creatures, how can we ourselves survive? We humans are most special when we work together to solve the problems we've created on planet earth.

Are we afraid to believe that we are a lot like the great apes? Stories about the beast hidden inside humans (like Dr. Jekyll and Mr. Hyde) have always been popular. . .and scary! Many people get very upset when scientists say that humans and apes had a common ancestor long ago. Perhaps that's because humans tend to project their own worse side on others. When you think about war, pollution, and crime, the great apes should be afraid to be like humans!

Nonhuman primates are a human's best friend. They were rocketed into space before human astronauts ever looked down at planet earth. Scientists use monkeys to learn how diseases are passed from human parents to their children. A monkey aided in the discovery of human blood types. And when scientists study nonhuman primate behavior, they gain insight into our human behavior.

PRIMATES

This glossarized index will help you find specific primate information. It will also help you understand the meaning of some of the words used in this book.

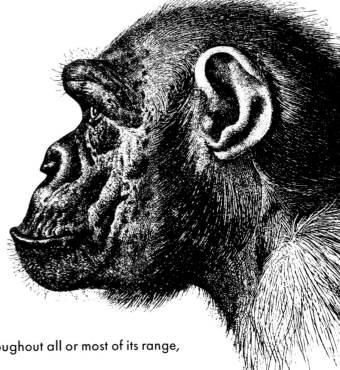

BOOKS FOR YOUNG READERS AGES 8 AND UP

from *John Muir Publications*

X-ray Vision Series

Each title in the series is 8¹/₂" x 11", 48 pages, $9.95, paperback, with four-color photographs and illustrations and written by Ron Schultz.

Looking Inside the Brain
Looking Inside Cartoon Animation
Looking Inside Sports Aerodynamics
Looking Inside Sunken Treasure
Looking Inside Telescopes and the
  Night Sky

Masters of Motion Series

Each title in the series is 10¹/₄" x 9", 48 pages, $9.95, paperback, with four-color photographs and illustrations.

How to Drive an Indy Race Car
  David Rubel
How to Fly a 747
  Tim Paulson
How to Fly the Space Shuttle
  Russell Shorto

The "Extremely Weird" Series

All of the titles are written by Sarah Lovett, 8¹/₂" x 11", 48 pages, and $9.95 paperbacks.

Extremely Weird Bats
Extremely Weird Birds
Extremely Weird Endangered Species
Extremely Weird Fishes
Extremely Weird Frogs
Extremely Weird Insects
Extremely Weird Primates
Extremely Weird Reptiles
Extremely Weird Sea Creatures
Extremely Weird Spiders

Other Titles of Interest

Habitats
Where the Wild Things Live
Randi Hacker and Jackie Kaufman
8¹/₂" x 11", 48 pages, color illustrations,
$9.95 paper

The Indian Way
*Learning to Communicate with
Mother Earth*
Gary McLain
Painting by Gary McLain
Illustrations by Michael Taylor
7" x 9", 114 pages, two-color illustrations,
$9.95, paper

**Kids Explore America's African-American
Heritage**
Westridge Young Writers Workshop
7" x 9", 112 pages, illustrations and
photographs, $8.95, paper

Kids Explore America's Hispanic Heritage
Westridge Young Writers Workshop
7" x 9", 112 pages, illustrations and
photographs, $7.95, paper

Rads, Ergs, and Cheeseburgers
*The Kids' Guide to Energy and the
Environment*
Bill Yanda
Illustrated by Michael Taylor
7" x 9", 108 pages, two-color illustrations,
$13.95, paper

The Kids' Environment Book
What's Awry and Why
Anne Pedersen
Illustrated by Sally Blakemore
7" x 9", 192 pages, two-color illustrations,
$13.95, paper

The Quill Hedgehog Adventure Series

Green fiction for young readers. Each title is written by John Waddington-Feather and illustrated by Doreen Edmond.

Quill's Adventures in the Great Beyond
BOOK ONE
5¹/₂" x 8¹/₂", 96 pages, $5.95, paper

Quill's Adventures in Wasteland
BOOK TWO
5¹/₂" x 8¹/₂", 132 pages, $5.95, paper

Quill's Adventures in Grozzieland
BOOK THREE
5¹/₂" x 8¹/₂", 132 pages, $5.95, paper

The Kidding Around Travel Guides

All of the titles listed below are 64 pages and $9.95 except for *Kidding Around the National Parks* and *Kidding Around Spain*, which are 108 pages and $12.95.

"A combination of practical information, vital statistics, and historical asides."
—New York Times

Kidding Around Atlanta
Kidding Around Boston, 2nd ed.
Kidding Around Chicago, 2nd ed.
Kidding Around the Hawaiian Islands,
Kidding Around London
Kidding Around Los Angeles
Kidding Around the National Parks
  of the Southwest
Kidding Around New York City, 2nd ed.
Kidding Around Paris
Kidding Around Philadelphia
Kidding Around San Diego
Kidding Around San Francisco
Kidding Around Santa Fe
Kidding Around Seattle
Kidding Around Spain
Kidding Around Washington, D.C., 2nd ed.